AF478552

FREEDOM AND MORALITY:

A NONSUBJECTIVE MORAL CODE

FREEDOM AND MORALITY:

A NONSUBJECTIVE MORAL CODE

by
Michel Anselme

Philosophical Library

New York

Library of Congress Cataloging in Publication Data

Anselme, Michel.
   Freedom and morality.

   1. Ethics. 2. Social ethics. I. Title.
BJ1012.A56 1983   170'.40   83-2465
ISBN 0-8022-2414-8

Translated from the original French *La Morale effective* by
Susan Wald.

CONTENTS

I. AN IMMUTABLE ETHIC

II. A RELATIVE MORALITY

SECTION ONE: LIFE AND DEATH

SECTION TWO: HAVING AND BEING

SECTION THREE: MAN AND HIS FELLOW MAN

III. A COMMON MINIMUM

PREFACE

Raised as a devout and practicing Catholic, I lost my faith at the age of thirty-two. Until then, sheltered by my convictions, I had no need to delve into questions of morality—God supplied an answer to everything. A believer, whatever his religion, knows beyond a doubt that he must not kill, slander, or steal because that is God's will or revealed word.

Since then, navigating without a compass, I, like many others, have had to find justification for my actions without any firm principles to guide me. I can attest that anyone who embarks on this solitary voyage without further reliance on metaphysical postulates is irredeemably alone — for the answers to his questions are nowhere to be found.

To one who has known faith, Dostoyevsky's exclamation — "If God is dead, everything is permitted" — is hardly surprising. When the foundations of moral laws collapse, he who no longer believes will naturally exclaim that the laws no longer exist! Since nothing is to be taken for granted any more, there is no reason to pick one action over another. It is quite true that to this freed prisoner, everything suddenly appears to be permitted.

The individual soon discovers, however, that no greater freedom is allowed, even to one whose God is dead. The existence of others limits his freedom, which he once believed to be his exclusive domain, although he cannot figure out why and how. I was long shaken by this realization; I had been convinced that, up to then, my actions had been governed solely by my faith.

The question of how my conduct might still be regulated once it had been freed of what I used to consider its sole restraint has continually occurred to me since then, and I have constantly tried to come up with suitable answers.

*   *
*

Moralists are not in short supply. Yet we are compelled to recognize, like Lévy-Bruhl, that while all accept the existence of a moral law, no one provides justification for it. He who seeks a foundation for morality and cannot find it by the metaphysical route will not be any more satisfied with ideological and philosophical theories; they are all equally barren in this respect. Having realized the futility of basing my investigations on speculative hypotheses, I turned in my quest to works dealing with aspects of human reality — paleontology, ethnology, ethology, biology, archaeology, and history.

Gradually, the idea emerged that would become the core of my approach. Converging toward it were the initial elements that now constitute the main thrust of my theory. If matter and life — because they are separate phenomena — conform to physical and biological laws that are specific to them, human consciousness — which is another distinct phenomenon — must necessarily conform to its own law. This law can neither be invented nor deduced from metaphysical, ideological, or philosophical theories. It can only be discovered in the observable realities of the phenomenon we call conscious life, just as the laws of physics and biology were discovered in the observable realities of matter and life.

Just as physics and biology express specific behaviors of matter and of living things, the law of consciousness must necessarily express the specific behavior of the conscious being, in other words, the conduct issuing from freedom, which is the human prerogative. Therefore, just as matter conforms to physical laws and life to biological laws, human consciousness must conform to moral laws.*

On completing my observations, I concluded that a type of moralism that attempts to set forth rules of conduct to be followed under all circumstances is invalid; but I also concluded that a variable and relative morality may be founded on an immutable ethic, the values of which must be weighed according to the situation.

I likewise concluded that human beings are without rights. By this I do not mean that human beings have not gotten the rights they are entitled to, but that they cannot lay claim to any rights at birth. Our societies were wrongly founded on the cultivation of rights, and the time has come to establish the cultivation of duty instead.

As our species has gone beyond its purely biological state to reach a state of consciousness, the role of physical evolution has given way to a cultural evolution that is making humanity less and less "animalistic" and more and more conscious, that is, more and more "humanized." This new type of evolution is also creating conditions that call for a real cultivation of duty to replace the earlier cultivation of rights.

What humanity needs now for its further humanization is neither a declaration of the rights of man nor a league for human rights, but a declaration and a league for human duties. There never was and never will be any validity to the notion of a right inherent in human nature, whereas human duties are inherent as soon as the signs of consciousness appear.

*The word "consciousness" is here defined very precisely as "a faculty exclusive to human beings of anticipating the outcome of their actions and judging them according to a concept of good and evil."

This is the reason why attempts to base morality on the cultivation of rights were, are, and will remain doomed to failure; for what we call the "rights of the individual" are nothing but the result of the duties of all. Duty is inherent in the nature of human beings, the only beings to have overcome nature; stated flatly, it is the basis of human morality, as well as the consequence of it.

INTRODUCTION

The discussion that follows aims to show:

1. That morality has a basis;
2. That it varies according to circumstances;
3. That is nevertheless conforms to inalienable, immutable, and universal principles;
4. That these principles constitute the law of conscious life;
5. That morality lays the basis for the humanization of humanity;
6. That it is independent of all idealism, metaphysics, and philosophy.

$$* \quad *$$
$$*$$

After giving thought to the matter, I claim that morality has a *basis*, whereas after more than twenty-five centuries of investigation, the greatest minds have resigned themselves to the contrary...I am perfectly aware of the impertinence of this statement.

I was, naturally, the first to be skeptical of the validity of my assertion. The explanation of my stubborness in pursuing an apparently senseless investigation lies in the idea — which seems irrefutable to me — that morality cannot *fail* to have a basis. Actually, observation shows unequivocally, on the one hand, that the immutable rule of the universe is to endow each phenomenon with a law of its own; and on the other hand, that consciousness cannot be reduced to mere physical and biological data. Thus consciousness is evidently a phenomenon, and like any phenomenon, must have its own law.

If my theory has flaws, they may have to do with the conclusions I draw from this fundamental notion, but not in any way with the legitimacy of the assertion — now hard to refute — that morality has a necessary basis.

This explains the stubbornness of my lengthy search or what might appear to be impossible, and my conviction that there is now no longer any brashness in setting forth my theory.

Hundreds of moral theories have been expounded, and one must ask why no one has shown that morality is based on a law of its own and not on personal opinions.

The answer appears rather clear if one looks closely at the twists and turns of thinking about morality through the centuries. Actually, while theories abound and it may seem surprising that none of them has ever attained its goal, history shows that this abundance is an illusion. In fact, there have never been more than two kinds of approaches to morality.

The first consists of finding a first principle from which the rules of conduct are derived. Whether this first principle is God or the gods, pleasure or altruism, happiness or solidarity, the approach is the same, and Lévy-Bruhl was correct in saying that they all constituted "metamoralities" which were equally incapable of serving as a basis for morality. Since the chosen principle involves the definition of immutable and universal rules of conduct, these rules could never conform to human realities, which are characterized by being evolutive and diversified.

The second approach, based on conclusions from the foregoing, leads to the impossibility of establishing a rule of conduct and culminates in the science of manners. It is therefore limited to observing everyday conduct, and the only conclusions it draws are those of "real-life" morality.

In the final analysis, the theory of a nonsubjective ethic is merely a third approach. It does not come after hundreds of great minds have tried in vain to explore possible bases for morality; it comes after hundreds of great minds have explored only two paths — the method of metamoralities and the observation of everyday life. Nonsubjective morality is not the product of any special genius; it merely opens up a new path not hitherto explored.

*   *
*

Despite the diversity of schools of thought, all have merely formulated *opinions*; not one has ever tried to find a *law* of consciousness, independent of a subjective principle chosen a priori.

No school of thought has hitherto searched for a *law of morality*, as in other times the first physicists searched for the law of physics. And we would never have known the laws of physics if the physicists had not eventually given up the opinions they had of it and systematicaliy discovered its laws. The originality of nonsubjective morality, which will, perhaps, allow it to succeed where other approaches have failed, lies in the attempt — as in physics and biology — to move away from opinion and into the realm of law.

*   *
*

Let us look more closely at the propositions of these various schools of thought.

15

We had and still have the *theological moralities*. Despite their number, they can all be summed up in the same way: from God — or the gods — all else flows. It was God who decided that man should do good, and it was He who spelled out what that good should consist of. Since these rules are immutable, they come directly under Lévy-Bruhl's justified reproof.

It is not a matter of condemning faith; it is simply a matter of admitting that there can be no connection between faith, which is immutable, and changing rules of conduct. Given this defect — and leaving aside the problem of faith — other theories of morality were bound to arise.

We then had the *moralities of sentiment*, which may also be summed up in the same way. God has not spelled out our duties, but in each individual, a sentiment has been instilled — by God, according to some; by nature, according to others — that can show him what is good and what is evil.

To be sure, there is much disagreement over the nature of this sentiment which urges man to do good; but whether it is sympathy (Adam Smith), pity (Schopenhauer), or altruism (Auguste Comte), it is always the same theory, in which a sentiment is chosen as the immutable and universal first principle from which flow equally immutable and universal rules — incompatible, therefore, with a diversified, perpetually evolving human race. Despite their seeming diversity, it is indeed always the same intellectual approach, which could never serve as a basis for morality. As a matter of fact, observation has shown that human conduct was never guided by a *single* sentiment, but on the contrary, by sentiments that varied remarkably according to the times, places, and groups, as well as for each individual according to the circumstances.

Moralities of willful intuition were then expounded. In this case, it is no longer a sentiment placed in each individual by

God or nature that instinctively leads him to good, but an intuition of the will; Descartes went so far as to say that it enables us to grasp "the true value of good." This position leads to the notion that intuition has its own forms of wisdom and that will transforms them into impulses for good. Unfortunately, any theory that relies on internal impulses — whether stemming from a sentiment, an intuition, or from will — were necessarily doomed to failure, for observation has shown that there are evil, as well as good, impulses.

With Kant, the notion of duty becomes a *categorical imperative*. He believed that reason, in and of itself, was capable of determining the rules of morality. But these rules decreed by our reason come into conflict with the tendencies of each individual. A rule is needed, therefore, to legislate in favor of good, for our tendencies could make us confuse it with evil. This rule is to act in such a way that the action could be adopted as a universal law by all reasonable beings. However, since Kant was never able to prove the impossibility of immoral rules of conduct being adopted by all reasonable beings, the "categorical imperative" soon became merely one more opinion.

Then came the *moralities of emotion*. These are based on the fact that any action creates an emotional state, and that moral choice is limited to choosing the action that produces the best emotional state. But whether these schools are hedonist, Cyrenaic, Epicurean, utilitarian, or positivist; whether they choose pleasure, pleasure in the fullest sense, individual happiness, or collective happiness; whether the pleasures are calculated mathematically, as with Bentham, or influenced by their quality, with J. Stuart Mill; whether, as with Spencer, happiness is one of the duties created by society, etc. — it is, once again, the same approach as in the moralities of sentiment, and fails for the same reasons.

Finally, we had the *moralities of values*, which sought to

establish a hierarchy of interrelated values. But any classification of values is subjective, for as Ribot wrote: "there can be no evaluation without a subject which evaluates." Thus, any theoretical classification of values was doomed to failure, for the choice of values necessarily rested on a priori opinion and could not represent the slightest progress over earlier attempts.

Regardless of what was chosen as the first principle, therefore — whether God, the gods, or altruism; virtue or sympathy; pleasure or happiness; the categorical imperative or the impulse of sentiment; the hierarchy of values or the intuition of will — the approach remained the same, namely, the *arbitrary choice of a precept* that had no better reason than any other to be chosen. This gave Lévy-Bruhl every right to say that this kind of approach — whether based on metaphysics or on a precept chosen a priori — always led to "metamoralities," which, stemming from a single principle, were necessarily incapable of serving as a rule of conduct for a diversified, evolving human race. Since 1902 he has never been proved wrong on this point.

*　　*
*

Having disposed of the first approach, we now come to the second. Once again, despite their differences, all the schools of thought set out on one and the same path and eventually led to the science of manners, in other words, the recognition that it is impossible to establish a rule of conduct and that one may as well be satisfied with observing morality as it is practiced.

The first ideas expressed in this new approach were those of *immediate experience*, and the doctrines of *moral experience*, such as those of Frederic Rauh. His view was that since each person is always finding himself in new situations, generalizations are useless; one should therefore free oneself

18

of all theories and seek conviction in immediate adaptation to reality, rather than deducing it from abstract ideologies.

Next came the *sociological attempts*, such as Durkheim's; aware of the confusion wrought by the disappearance of rules of conduct, he sought a remedy and believed he had found it in the rigorously scientific study of society. Hence, through methodical experiment, one aims to grasp social facts in order to arrive at a social rule. Convinced that a permanent rule that enables society to last is a proof of that rule's validity, he thus opened the way to those who would postulate that there is only one given morality, that which can be studied by science as a fact, and that mores — always relative to a given society — can only be observed.

With this method — and although there were many schools — there was, once again, only a single type of approach. Gurwich summarized this approach very well when he wrote that a theoretical morality can now only be limited to the description of the concrete variations of the morality that is practiced on an everyday basis.

From the metamoralities that were unable to establish a basis for morality, we have now come to the outright denial of morality as a rule of conduct.

*　　*
*

Upon completing my investigation, I realize that, in common with the metamoralists, I believe that a basis can be established for morality. But I deeply disagree with their approach. Whether one believes that the first principle is God, happiness, altruism, pleasure, or virtue, one must first be a "believer" in order to accept the rules of conduct that may derive from it. For to put virtue, happiness, pleasure, or altruism, as well as God or the gods, as the supreme rule is to be a believer.

19

The theory of a nonsubjective ethic which I feel qualified to set forth is in absolute contradiction with the metamoralists, who believe that an immutable law of conduct may issue from a first principle chosen according to their own belief or opinion. But this ethic is in even greater disagreement with those systems that lead to the impossibility of morality, since the entire theory of a nonsubjective ethic rests on the fact that the law of consciousness cannot fail to exist from the instant that the phenomenon of consciousness is observed.

The metamoralities, despite their errors, have served humanity well, on the whole; it is because of them that human conduct has not been worse. But what can be expected from a denial of morality? Or from a "morality" that is limited to the observation of manners? The risk, quite simply, is that blatantly immoral conduct will be legitimized. If we accept the idea that a situation has only to exist in order to be deemed moral, then if there are ten times as many concentration camps or gulags in the world, their morality will be ten times greater! These theories are bringing us a little closer each day to the notion that "everything is permitted"; they tend to foster the idea that human beings can enjoy rights without being subject to any obligations. Although relatively new, they have already fostered a great deal of confusion among contemporary thinkers.

They are also having a great impact on philosophy. It is no accident that the philosophers of the absurd have enjoyed such popularity in recent times. If Sartre could state that being is its own nothingness, and if Marcuse could dare to assert that instinct leads to liberation from social discontent through death, Hartmann preached collective suicide long before, and first-century Mahayanism — preceding Freud, Sartre, and Marcuse — also asserted the identity of being and nothingness, and the liberating power of death.

These ideas — that since the human being is nothing, he has no need of morality — are as old as the world itself, but they are finding greater acceptance today, in a world increasingly in disarray, in which what is often merely paradoxical or absurd is considered ''modern'' by pseudo-intellectuals.

The nonsubjective ethic intends to open a new path; every new step will always be more ''modern'' than the current outmoded ideas about being-equals- nothingness and death-as-a-liberator. May those who claim they want to live, while wishing to be nothing, remain smug in their speculations.

*   *
*

Moral guideposts exist today only for those whose beliefs stem from theological moralities. But it must be acknowledged that these guideposts are being uprooted faster and faster by scientific questioning and by the growing gap between immutable rules and changing reality. In the realm of morality, theology is retreating and is fighting only rearguard battles. For how long will it continue to satisfy its most faithful followers *on the level of morality*, regardless of the persistence of faith? Yet is is urgent, once again, that a parent be able to answer his children, that a person in doubt be able to tell good from evil, and that judges have a system on which to base equitable decisions, even if they are not satisfied or are no longer satisfied with a theological morality whose immutable nature is increasingly in conflict with the ever variable reality.

The role of a nonsubjective ethic is to formulate the law of consciousness — rather than another opinion — so that, while always in keeping with the realities of human nature, it can respond — whatever the outcome may be — to the confusion left by the failure of the metamoralities and the consequence of that failure, the science of manners which resulted in the denial of morality itself.

Rigid moralism has proven its inability to serve as a basis for human conduct. For this reason it is increasingly distrusted and neglected. The time has come to proceed to weigh the values of an "ethicism" capable of formulating moral answers by adapting to the circumstances, thus overcoming the present absurd situation, which can lead only to complete permissiveness. This would be an intolerable situation for humanity, which cannot survive without norms. Observation has long since shown that a society without norms is destined to vanish.

I

AN IMMUTABLE ETHIC

I. A SPECIFIC LAW OF CONSCIOUS LIFE

Each state has its specific law. Molecules behave according to their own principles; when several molecules come together to form a cell, that cell has its own law which is not the same as for molecules. Matter conforms to physical laws; living things conform to biological laws. In the same way, consciousness must conform to its own law.

The fact that each state observes a specific law is an immutable rule in our universe. To deny that consciousness necessarily conforms to its own law, one would have to show that consciousness is not a specific phenomenon — that it does not differ in any respect from matter or from non-conscious life, which would be patently absurd — or that each observable phenomenon in the universe does not always conform to its own specific law, which would be in utter contradiction to experience.

A law of conduct specific to beings possessing consciousness *cannot fail to exist*, given that such beings exist in our universe.

If we were able to perceive the existence of consciousness separate from living things, we would be scientifically justified in seeking its law in a purely spiritual context. But given our inability to observe the existence of consciousness outside of human beings, we are compelled to search for the law of consciousness in the narrow, specific context of that consciousness's embodiment.

Thus, the law of consciousness must cover the full range of human experience — the experience of "living consciousness" — from the time that the first hominid began to think before acting, until the last man acts deliberately and with reason for the last time.

Heretofore the rules of morality have been formulated according to opinions. Thus we are constantly seeing these rules challenged whenever opinion is overruled by the acquisition of new knowledge.

The law of consciousness cannot be derived from opinion, any more than the laws of physics or biology. Therefore, it must be *researched* and *discovered*, as were the principles of physics and biology.

It is well established today that the earliest hominids differed less from the prehominid primates than the latter did from their own ancestors. We are therefore justified in assuming that the morality of the earliest human groups essentially flowed from natural mechanisms which could not easily be disobeyed. We further conclude that the morality we observe today among various human groups is the result of changes gradually introduced by disobeying instinctive behaviors. In other words, the morality that can be observed today is the result of the victory of freedom over determinism.

An integral part of the human adventure, morality evolves with it, moving away from its early naturalness like humanity itself. It therefore changes incessantly.

Moreover, since various human groups have not evolved at the same pace, their rules of morality differ not only according to epochs, but also, depending on the group, according to their environment and level of evolution.

Morality thus appears as having always been and remaining fundamentally *variable* and *relative*.

*   *
*

2. AN IMMUTABLE ETHIC

Humanity went through a long initial period during which morality was essentially made up of behaviors inherited from the higher mammals. The value of this "natural morality" should not be underestimated; everything flows from it, not only the continuation and betterment of the species, but also the first expressions of human solidarity and the first victories of freedom over determinism. Nothing suggests that the moralities of opinion have been able to do as much.

By arbitrarily selecting a principle and then defining the rules for obeying it, the moralities of opinion were doomed to be immutable and universal. They thus showed themselves to be incompatible with the real conduct of a human race characterized by evolution and diversity.

It is true, therefore, that morality has no basis, if what is meant thereby is that it is not based on a theory of opinion.

25

But it is false if what is meant is that it has no basis. Morality, defined as the law of conscious life, asserts itself independently of any theory of opinion from the moment that the phenomenon of living consciousness makes its appearance in the universe, just as the laws of physics and biology assert themselves from the instant that matter and life appear. This is solely because any particular phenomenon is always associated with its own law.

Just as the laws of physics and biology could not be anything but immutable, the law of conscious life cannot be variable and relative. Yet, as we have seen, invariable moralities are incompatible with humanity, which is particularly characterized by evolution and diversity.

The contradiction appears irreconcilable; it is, however, not as it appears. The variant applications of the law should not be confused with the inalienability of its principles. A lever of *relative* size is necessary to move an object of relative weight placed at a relative distance from its point of support. Immutable as they are, the laws of physics themselves cause different reactions depending on the situation.

Just like the laws of physics and biology, the law of conscious life can merely pronounce the *immutable* rules, which when applied are likely to produce as many *variable* and *relative* responses as there are situations.

The term NONSUBJECTIVE ETHIC will refer to the immutable, universal law of conscious life, which in the framework of the human adventure, governs the thinking of all human beings in whatever group, in all periods, in all environments, in all circumstances, and regardless of the situation. *Ethic*, because it is the ''science of morality'' and the ''art of regulating conduct''; *nonsubjective*, because it exists in reality, independent of our ideas of it.

The term NONSUBJECTIVE MORALITY will refer to the

modes of conduct in their practical application, hence variable and relative, that conform to the nonsubjective ethic.

*　　*

*

3. A PRINCIPLE OF FREEDOM, EQUITY, AND TRUTH

Just as the laws of physics and biology result from the specific nature of matter and life, the ethical law must necessarily result from the specific nature of conscious life. Montesquieu was the first to point this out: "Law is but the expression of the thing." If we want a chance to perceive the law of conscious life, we must therefore first state its characteristic. We know from the evidence that the special feature of human consciousness is the faculty, and even the vital necessity, of making choices. If animal conduct results essentially from genetic *programming*, human conduct is not programmed. To be more precise, our programming takes the form of impulses and is limited to confronting us with choices. Each person is left to control his own impulses on his own responsibility. In other words, what characterizes human conduct is the necessity and obligation to choose. Everything that surrounds us — from the cosmos to the atom, from the highest animal to the lowliest plant — obeys rigid programming and cannot make the least choice. Everything but human consciousness conforms to determinism.

There is only one choice that humans cannot make: to refuse to choose. For a human being, refusing to choose is a categorical choice that amounts to shedding his characteristic feature. It is a choice that amounts to giving up his humanity. Thus, the essential characteristic of human consciousness, its specific nature which it shares with no other, is revealed beyond all possible questioning to be *freedom*.

27

It is by making use of that freedom that man departs from his animal origin and establishes that he is his own master, responsible for his fate and sharing responsibility for the fate of humanity. Therefore, we are justified in recognizing freedom as not only the characteristic of conscious life, but the first principle of its law as well.

However, freedom would no longer be a principle if its exercise by some resulted in curtailing that of others. It would become a privilege associated with power, exercised at the expense of weakness. Therefore, to remain a principle, freedom absolutely implies the existence of *equity*. However, if knowledge of the facts of a situation are lacking, an equitable decision is impossible. Therefore, there can be no moral debate apart from the search for *truth*. It follows that if freedom is the first principle of the law of consciousness, equity and truth must necessarily be its two complementary principles.

*　　*
*

4. AN OBLIGATION TO THE SPECIES

The visible universe has given no evidence of the existence of consciousness apart from human beings. We can state, therefore, that the extinction of the human species would mean the disappearance of the only example of consciousness hitherto observed.

Thus consciousness, in order to preserve itself, must perforce *preserve* the human species. This fact is the basis of the obligation to preserve the species which is incumbent on every living, conscious being.

Species are ruled by simple mechanisms which enable them to *survive* and to *adapt*. They guarantee their survival by aiming to safeguard each group, and, if possible, each individual.

They guarantee their adaptation by adopting "beneficial" mutations and increasing the number of "the fittest" — those best adapted or more adaptable — at the expense of the "less fit", those less adaptable or adapted.

But the conscious species, which has the option of disobedience, cannot avoid the question of whether it will decide to obey or disobey the natural processes in order to insure its continued existence.

Thus, each thinking being must face the question of whether or not he will take part in the survival of humanity. First and foremost, he must decide whether or not to contribute to his own survival.

This is not strictly a matter of morality. Given the existence of human beings, morality guides their behavior. To expound the reasons for being or not being is not within its province. It is merely obvious that the extinction of human beings would render useless the notion of morality by eliminating questions about human behavior, just as the extinction of living beings would render useless the notion of biology.

Given the existence of human beings, questions regarding their behavior cannot escape notice. In spite of the philosophers of the absurd, professing that since nothing leads to anything, nothing is worth trying, their argument cannot convince us: for by formulating it they chose to be, hence to conduct themselves in a certain way.

Even if the human experience were nothing but a transient accident devoid of any purpose, the specific law of human behavior exists, just as the laws of physics and biology exist independently of the purposefulness, or lack thereof, of matter and life. Therefore we are justified in stating that as long as a conscious human species has existed and exists, its behavior is and will continue to be rooted in moral laws that constitute its particular law. We are likewise justified in stating that this law applies to every human being, regardless of the ways in which he may recoil from the necessity of being, so long as he remains alive and conscious.

In its early stages, the human species was nearly wholly preoccupied by the difficulties it had to overcome merely in order to survive, and therefore did not seriously violate its obligations as a species. Respectful of the moral rules arising from the instinctual mechanisms inherited from the higher mammals, mankind was long able to survive and adapt naturally, without much wracking of its conscience.

The modern era, on the other hand, has revealed the conflict between freedom and the obligation to the species. Mankind today is swerving more and more frequently onto paths inimical to its own survival, and in general, is doing so without having clearly chosen to.

To be sure, any disobedience to instinctual mechanisms, i.e., to determinism, is an assertion of freedom and may be interpreted as a victory of consciousness. But while disobedience to the natural mechanisms has hitherto enabled the species to survive and adapt, it can just as easily lead to the extinction of mankind, and, by extension, to the disappearance of consciousness, hence of liberty. The reason for this is simple: no freedom has been observed apart from conscious life; no conscious life has been observed apart from the human species; and without respect for its natural mechanisms, any species is in danger of extinction.

The conscious species will obviously not experience the obligation imposed upon it as a matter of fate. It must think things out before accepting the necessity of it. Furthermore, it is only through reason that one can achieve one's true goals without letting oneself be deceived by apparent goals, as happens when instinct is followed — as, for example, when the swarming locust, believing that it is saving itself and its group, flies straight ahead to its doom. Notions of secondary and long-term consequences are absent from instinctual drives.

Thus, despite the identity of outcomes, and the fact that it may be formulated in the same way for the nonconscious as for the conscious being, the *obligation to the species* is not of the same nature. The obligation of the former is imposed by way of determinism, and can therefore involve neither choice nor responsibility. The latter, however, fully entails responsibility and is inseparably linked to the ethic and its principle of freedom.

The obligation to take part in the survival and adaptation of the human species *therefore constitutes a limitation on the freedom of individual consciousness and is the primary moral obligation arising from its embodiment.*

*   *
*

5. A SOCIAL OBLIGATION

Although matter, life and consciousness conform to specific laws, scientific observation has shown that they are all governed by a single law of evolution through the stages of integration. From the simpler to the more complex, the stages consist of integration at the level of the molecule, then the cell, then the metazoon (i.e., multicellular animals), and finally, of society.

Each level is integrated into a higher one by accepting the constraints of exchange, relationship, information, organization and hierarchy.

Thus, individual consciousnesses which were totally isolated from one another, refusing all exchange, all relationship, all information and all hierarchical and organizational constraint would never come under a common law of behavior, because, in such a case, their freedom would not come into conflict with the freedom of others, any more than molecules which were totally isolated from one another and not combined into a cell could be governed by the laws that regulate the functioning of a cell.

The fact that the units of conscious life are *integrated* at the social level, the fact that men form societies, means that their conduct does come under the law which is specific to them. In like fashion, each particular state has its law, each stage of integration has its laws. Observation of the molecule, the cell and the metazoon testifies to this, as does observation of the special bonds between man and mankind.

Whereas animal young inherit at birth the mere genetic transmission of their inborn nature, the human child receives from his group all that distinguishes him from a higher mammal. Children who have been raised by animals supply proof of this.

Thus, man is what he is solely because human society has passed on to him its gains, because it has transmitted acquired culture in addition to the biological inheritance.

A person who can add "I am" to the statement "I think" owes that ability to the care and concern of humanity. The transmission of the cultural capital is what enables men to succeed men. If humanity were limited to transmitting its genetic capital, it would produce only huge naked apes, capable of becoming men, of course, but destined not to do so.

Thus, man as a conscious being is the product of his society, not his species. Therefore, the bonds between man and mankind are of a very special nature, for to each person society is both parent and child: having given him all, it must be given all in return in order to survive. Interdependence is total. If the bonds were undone, we would not have men, on the one hand, and humanity on the other, but merely a group of huge mammals.

Hence, for its own self-preservation, consciousness must preserve both the human species and its societies. Therefore, *the social obligation, like the obligation to the species, is an absolute moral obligation.*

*   *

*

6. A TACIT CONTRACT

The transmitted gain is the result of efforts made and accumulated from the time when humanity emerged. It is the work of those who struggled to give back to humanity more than they had received from it, the result of the sacrifice of unknown ancestors who were mistreated by an implacable Nature. The social gain has grown from the earliest awakening of thought to the enormous cultural capital of our time. It is this freely transmitted viaticum which makes man a conscious being. Thus man has contracted a fundamental debt which has enabled him to exist.

Thus, a tacit, fundamental pact exists between man and humanity. If he does not repay his debt, man breaks the pact. In so doing, he becomes a thief, unworthy of the credit granted to him, for it was granted only so that he might pass it on in turn.

Whoever consents to be cannot deny his debt. Each person faces a single question: repay, or disappear.

Furthermore, voluntary extinction is not a neutral act but rather an assault on the humanization process.

In the nakedness of birth, man can have no rights. No rights inherent in human nature will ever be proved. Obviously, whoever can add "I am" to the statement "I think" will never be anything but a debtor. But can he ever repay what he owes to those he owes it to? Life, to his progenitors, and education to his teachers? Obviously not. For that matter, teachers and parents are merely the appointees of humanity, charged with granting a loan in its name which they themselves have already received and are bound to repay.

The harvest does not give back the seed to past plantings. It pays its debt by supplying the seed of future harvests. Clearly, the advance which has been received should be paid back to those who need it in order that they may participate in turn in the humanization process.

I shall call the tacit contract based on social obligation the MORAL CONTRACT. From this moral contract is derived a principle of solidarity *which is as fundamental for humanity as is the obligation of survival and adaptation for a species. For without such solidarity, there can be no humanity.*

Thus is established what we will call the duty to participate in the humanization of humanity, in other words, that which enables humanity to move farther and farther each day away from its original animalism.

*   *
*

7. A NONSUBJECTIVE ETHIC

If freedom is the first principle of consciousness, but if consciousness, when it is associated with life, is constrained by equity, truth, the obligation to the species and the social obligation, we may then define the moral debate as that which arbitrates between five values which might otherwise be in opposition.

The moral debate leads to *arbitration* between opposing forces, and *the rules which govern conscious life result from the union of a principle of freedom which tends toward the absolute, but is narrowly controlled by its two intrinsic constraints — equity and truth — and by two obligations: the obligation to the species and the social obligation.*

In this way, the inalienable, immutable and universal principles of a nonsubjective ethic, which can enable the moral debate to adjust its response to each set of circumstances, may be formulated as follows:

1. a *principle of freedom,* namely
    a. the voluntary, deliberate decision to oppose or cooperate with the determining factors,
    b. within the limits of the obligation to the species,
    c. within the limits of the social obligation,
    d. with respect for equity and truth.

—

2. An *obligation to the species,* namely
    a. the voluntary and deliberate decision to limit one's own freedom,
    b. in order to insure the survival of the species, the group and the individual,
    c. in order to insure the adaptation of the species,
    d. taking into account the real immediate, long-term and secondary consequences,
    e. with respect for the social obligation and for equity and truth.

—

3. A *social obligation,* namely
    a. the voluntary and deliberate decision to limit one's own freedom:
    b. in order to contribute to the humanization of humanity by seeking to contribute more than one receives,
    c. in order to safeguard each individual and group within the limits of the obligation to the species,

    d. taking into account the real immediate, long-term and
secondary consequences,
    e. with respect for equity and truth.

—

4. A *constraint by equity*, namely
    a. to arbitrate conflicts with respect for equality in regard
to the freedom of each group and individual,
    b. with respect for their equal chances, and
    c. with respect for their equal treatment, assuming equal
merit.

—

5. A *constraint by truth*, namely
    a. to keep the moral debate within the strict framework
of real knowledge of the situation, and within the narrowest
possible framework of knowledge of goals and consequences.

*   *

*

The task of nonsubjective morality is to transpose the immutable law of the nonsubjective ethic into any number of
suitable answers to the circumstances of daily life, so that its
principles may be respected in a wide range of situations.

If a human group were threatened with extinction due to
underpopulation, morality would be commanded by the ethic
to condemn birth control, whereas if the same group were
threatened with extinction due to overpopulation, the same
principle would prescribe that excess fertility be condemned.

Since a moral rule that never varies in its application might
become immoral if the situation changes, the answers supplied by a nonsubjective morality must change whenever the
situation changes in order to respect the immutability of the
ethic.

Based directly on the realities of life and of consciousness, nonsubjective morality is rooted in no particular explanation of the universe, no metaphysic and no philosophy. To the contrary, respect for the nonsubjective ethic leads to the adoption of completely independent theories and ideals.

An ideal, because this ethic establishes morality as the principal element of humanization, for the simple reason that, without morality, there would be nothing but pre- or infrahumanity.

A theory, because it leads to the superiority of a common minimal morality over philosophies and metaphysics, for the simple reason that without morality there would be nothing but pre- or infrahumanity and therefore no philosophy or metaphysic.

But this ideal can neither be substituted for nor compared to the ideals of metaphysics, any more than their theory can be substituted for or compared to the theories of philosophy.

In adopting nonsubjective morality as the guiding principle of his life and in recognizing it as the motor element of humanization, man is merely submitting to his own law. Respect for this specific law does not conflict with any ideal that may be chosen by an individual, so long as it does not lead to disobeying the nonsubjective ethic.

Thus, the nonsubjective ethic establishes the autonomy of rules of conduct with respect to the debate on the priority of essence over existence, as well as whether there is a purpose to life, consciousness and humanity.

It may therefore be adopted utterly independent of any philosophy or metaphysic. Since nonsubjective morality is the expression of a law, not of an opinion, it is incumbent first and foremost on everyone. Philosophies, ideologies and metaphysics are nothing but secondary, individual and optional choices.

II

A RELATIVE MORALITY

Note: While the purpose of the first chapter of this book is to set forth a theory, the chapter which follows consists essentially of examples. It aims to show how the five principle/values of the ethic may be combined with circumstances. For every different circumstance described, the moral solution changes. In the final analysis, therefore, there is only one indicative value.

SECTION ONE: LIFE AND DEATH

1. VOLUNTARY DEATH

However sublime the theories, however oriented the metamoralities were toward supernatural ends, they could not escape the necessity of sanctifying life. The disdain for the flesh which was sometimes expressed did not lead to disdain for life.

In the perspective of the nonsubjective ethic, life wedded to consciousness constitutes the supreme value of humanity, for without conscious life the human being would not exist.

Thus, any act intended to put an early end to any conscious existence is a direct assault on the supreme value of humanity.

To adopt nonsubjective morality means first and foremost to reject any conduct which, were it universally adopted, would lead to the destruction or diminution of conscious life, i.e., to the destruction or diminution of the human species or of humanity. An attempt on a single conscious life is perforce an attempt on the species and on humanity. It violates the obligation to the species and the social obligation.

In terms of the obligation to the species and the social obligation, the respect for individual life, including one's own, is therefore an absolute obligation, for two reasons: 1. the group's survival depends on the survival of its individual members; 2. the *individual* repayment of the inherited debt is impossible unless *each* individual existence is preserved.

These same obligations, however, require certain lives to be sacrificed in certain exceptional circumstances, for example, in order to save others or to enable the group to go forward. It therefore appears that respect for each individual life is secondary to the needs for survival and humanization of the group itself.

Thus, if an individual has lost once and for all the faculties that enable him to contribute to humanization, his decision to put an early end to his life no longer has any relationship to the obligation to the species or to the social obligation, but is solely a matter of personal freedom. No restrictions apply except those that an individual may adopt within the framework of his *personal ethic.*

In the perspective of a nonsubjective ethic, and under normal circumstances, the practice of voluntary death is therefore utterly immoral, except in a case where the ability to contribute to humanization has been lost once and for all. Thus, voluntary euthanasia may be *moral, neutral or immoral, depending on the circumstances.*

When the recovery of one's faculties is uncertain but highly improbable, and the horror of one's situation leads anyway to the choice of death, two situations may arise:

— the inherited debts have not been acquitted and the moral contract has not been performed. In that case, choosing to die without having made every attempt to give back to humanity more than was received is tainted with immorality.

— the moral contract has been fulfilled. In that case, although it is more admirable to try to continue taking part in the humanization process — and thus be one of those who until they have given their all feel that they have given nothing — the nonsubjective ethic does not prescribe the obligation to do so.

But how can one claim to have fulfilled the contract? In the absence of real knowledge of a real situation, trying to distinguish a fulfilled moral contract from an unfulfilled one is very abstract. Likewise, it would be futile to attempt to set forth the conditions that could make voluntary death compatible with nonsubjective morality in the absence of a real situation displaying *exceptional* circumstances. The theoretical situations described herein have no other purpose than to demonstrate the reasoning which enables nonsubjective morality to respect the ethic by adapting to various situations.

*   *
*

2. THE COURTING OF RISK

In general, the metamoralities distinguish direct suicide, in which one kills oneself outright, from indirect suicide, in which one destroys oneself gradually, either voluntarily or by taking careless risks.

Nonsubjective morality is, of course, opposed both to indirect voluntary death and to the direct kind. And the circumstances which allow the taking of risks likely to incur death, without that being the intended goal, are therefore every bit as exceptional for indirect as for direct suicide. It is unnecessary to restate the priority of the obligation to the species and the social obligation; obviously, a person who accepts risks that are liable to incur his own death in order to save or bring progress to his group commits no immoral act, in contrast to one who sacrifices the group in order to save himself.

Doctors, rescuers or policemen who take risks in order to fight epidemics, save lives or protect them, *fulfill their duty by agreeing to place themselves in jeopardy.* However, the courting of risk by the bullfighter or racing-car driver arises from no exceptional circumstance and is therefore patently immoral.

A pilot who fails to make rigorous inspections, a driver who neglects to change worn tires, or a worker who disobeys safety regulations not only commit reckless and unprofessional errors; *they also commit wrongs against morality.*

For the same reason, personal grooming and care of one's health entail obligations. On an individual level, attention to diet, physical exercise and the avoidance of unhealthy practices are as much a part of morality as, on the collective level, housing, work cadences, transportation, urban development or medical facilities, which are, in fact, the means of public hygiene.

The use of medicine, vaccinations and surgery when they offer *real* statistical chances of improving physical health, *can therefore be seen as obligations.* By the same token, failure to isolate contagious diseases, or the transmission of defects to one's offspring — cross-generational contagion — *constitute assaults on public hygiene, hence on the species and on morality.*

Physical exercise which keeps the body in good condition meets moral requirements; however, sports competition may be in opposition to them if it leads to overexertion and excessive risks. In physical exercise, as in food and sexuality, there is a threshold above or below which physical equilibrium may suffer, in the short or long run. It is when this threshold is crossed that moral judgment must make a correction.

*   *
*

3. CHOOSING BETWEEN TWO LIVES

In the choice between two lives, the obligation to the species and the social obligation lead to preserving the one which has the greatest chances of making the best contribution to the humanization process.

It is not by accident that hunters spare female animals and their young, and that the rule in rescue operations is "women and children first." When game is scarce, and when population growth is the safest way to insure survival of the species, those lives richest in demographic potential are the ones that must be saved.

But everything changes if crops are threatened by the proliferation of game, as everything would change within a human group actually threatened with extinction as a result of overpopulation.

If Pasteur had drowned while trying to save a stranger before inventing his vaccine, he would have demonstrated his unselfishness, but he would have acted against the process of humanization. Of course, the fact that there is no way for anyone to know if he will turn out to be Pasteur someday, or if the stranger will not — in other words, the impossibility of judging the long-term consequences — ordinarily prevents the classification of lives according to their potential contributions.

But whenever exceptional circumstances make it possible to establish a definite hierarchy of potential contribution to humanization, assuming that a choice must be made between two lives, the nonsubjective ethic would choose the useful over the useless and ability over inability, solely from the perspective of which could make a greater contribution.

If before a child's birth, therefore, it becomes necessary to sacrifice the mother in order to save the child, nonsubjective morality dictates that only the mother should be saved. The unborn child, like the newborn, possesses nothing but its inherited capital. If kept apart from human society for a few years, they would never grow out of their animal nature. Whereas the mother fully meets the definition of a conscious being, they do not yet meet it and their lives are no more than potentially human.

The mother has already enjoyed the benefit of the transmitted wealth; it is now time for her to repay her debt. She contributes to humanization. There is no reason to deter her from fulfilling this duty by exchanging her life for that of a new creature to which society has not yet transmitted human characteristics. *When a choice must be made, the real ex-*

istence of conscious life and the real capacity to contribute to humanization must outweigh their mere potential.

*   *

*

4. THE RIGHT OF SUBSISTENCE

For each generation, the nonsubjective ethic renews the obligation to transmit the cultural wealth accumulated over thousands of centuries to each of those who will transmit it in turn. Should a single generation fail to do so, humanity would disappear as a species characterized by a culture and a consciousness formed in the course of several million years. This obligation is based on the debt incurred to previous generations, not on a right supposedly possessed by a newborn.

Thus, the interruption of pregnancy, or the failure to provide the medical aid necessary to save the life of a newborn which has been diagnosed as *completely* and *irreversibly* unfit to receive and transmit the legacy, would not constitute an immoral action. Since it is purely a question of biological life, only biological laws apply. Furthermore, since the proliferation of beings unfit to receive and transmit the legacy may represent a threat to the species, it may in some cases be immoral not to prevent this.

Of course, the principle of freedom allows each person to go beyond the demands of the nonsubjective ethic and prefer, in accordance with his personal ethic, to save the newly conceived or newborn creature, even if it is totally unfit to fulfill the obligations of conscious life. But whoever makes such a choice must personally assume its consequences, for he does so against the interests of the group, which cannot absorb an indefinite increase in subhuman lives without running the risk of extinction. In order to obey the obligation to the species, the group cannot accept the injunction to take the

45

responsibility for personal choices which are contrary to its interests. *If it were placed in jeopardy by the proliferation of subhuman lives, it would be forced to use authoritarian measures to put a stop to it.*

While humanity is absolutely obliged to transmit the legacy to those who can transmit it in turn, it has no such obligation with regard to those who are completely and irrevocably incompetent from the standpoint of consciousness.

But biological life, without which the existence of consciousness would not be observed, remains a fundamental value. A biological life which has received the care necessary to enable it to be born, though it may be completely unfit from the standpoint of consciousness, is therefore entitled at least to biological protection.

It is a different case with a conscious life that is only partially disabled. The smallest spark of consciousness joined to life carries the same obligations as conscious life.

Thus, the group is compelled to:
1. take full responsibility, from the cultural as well as the biological standpoint, for those who are partially unfit to fulfill their moral contract;
2. take responsibility, but only from the biological standpoint, for those who prove to be *irrevocably* disabled from the standpoint of consciousness, once medical care has enabled them to be born;
3. prevent the proliferation of subhuman lives.

*   *
*

The absence of any rights attaching to birth frees each generation from the obligation to take care of parasites, that is, those who are not disabled but refuse to take part in humanization. If they cannot attend to their own needs, the group from which they have withdrawn is in no way obligated to add to the advance which has already been wasted on them. *A group which was placed in jeopardy by such parasitism would be compelled to put a stop to it by authoritarian methods.*

Here the group's obligation is never to permit establishment of the unjust principle "to each according to his needs" — whereby some individuals who are not prevented from making a contribution would always take without ever giving, leading to a setback for humanization. It is likewise an obligation not to permit establishment of the sole principle "to each according to what he produces", which could lead to denying basic necessities to those who are *truly* prevented from contributing.

The notions of aid or charity toward the unfit who are *prevented* from contributing have no meaning from the standpoint of nonsubjective morality. *They must be cared for,* but such care is based on the *duties* incurred to previous generations, and in no way on any right attributed to the beneficiaries.

*   *

*

5. EUGENICS

Eugenics is said to be *positive* when it attempts to mold the characteristics of a population in the image of a preselected ideal, with the aim of improving it by cross-breeding and elimination.

We now know that the apparent improvement of populations through positive eugenics holds the gravest dangers for groups and species. Any standardization of the characteristics of their members, even if these may be considered the best ones, places them in jeopardy. The capacity for adaptation and resistance to attack lies precisely in diversity. Nature enables species to adapt and survive, not by standardizing them but rather by going so far as to make each individual unique.

Thus, even if it could be made compatible with freedom, *positive eugenics would still be immoral*, for the simple reason that it would eventually make the human species less and less adaptable and therefore less and less likely to survive.

Eugenics is said to be *negative* when it merely gives each individual the option of avoiding the hereditary transmission of possible defects. We now know how to affect the genetic transmission of bacteria, and it is plausible to imagine that this could be done for human beings. Since each person could freely avail himself of it, the application of negative eugenics to man would therefore be compatible with individual freedom, and would limit the proliferation of hereditary defects which might endanger the human species. It cannot, therefore, be accused of immorality. To the contrary, in many cases, *it might be immoral not to make use of it to fulfill the obligation to the species*.

A negative eugenics which could permit the improvement of the human species while respecting individual freedom is still only a distant hope. In the meantime, bearers of serious hereditary defects have the duty to avoid procreation. There is nothing immoral in deciding not to procreate in a world which is not threatened by underpopulation, whereas *it is gravely immoral to contribute to the enfeeblement of the species*. The obligation to participate in the improvement of the species perforce involves the duty to contribute to the improvement of one's own descendants, and to take actions which are likely to improve the descendants of one's group. Thus it is proper to work for the acquisition of new knowledge with regard to insuring favorable mutations and preventing the transmission of genetic defects. And it is not necessary to wait for new discoveries in order to obey, here and now, the simple rules already known which can contribute to improvement:

1. Since it is clearly established, for example, that children born to women aged 22 to 25 years are, on the average, healthier and have an average I.Q. 10-15 percent higher than children born to older women, and since it is clearly established that 80 percent of Mongoloid children are born to women over 40 years of age, it is moral to deprive the individual satisfactions of procreation in middle age.

2. Since it is clearly established that the diet of the Sikhs — to cite only a classic example — has produced a race more robust and resistant than its neighbors, it is moral to obey dietary rules which can improve one's descendants, etc.

In summary, it is moral to actively encourage science to rapidly provide better clues and new methods likely to help improve the human species, but *it would be immoral, in the meantime, not to obey, here and now, the elementary rules which can contribute to that end.*

*　　*
*

6. PROCREATION

If the group is likely to be endangered, or if its capacities for humanization threaten to recede as a result of underpopulation, the moral contract clearly imposes on every fit individual the duty to reproduce.

Life, which is the property of no one but is the usufruct of all, is perforce one of the primary obligations to be repaid. But as long as the group is growing or remains within satisfactory bounds, each person remains completely free to choose the means by which he fulfills his moral contract. No

49

one is compelled to repay the education he has received by becoming a teacher, just as no one is compelled to directly repay the life he has received, provided the group does not lack either teachers or parents.

Each person must repay his debt by contributing to the overall progress of the group in the ways in which he is best fitted to do so. Happy is he who can state at the close of his life that his contribution met the deepest needs of his group and his time.

If, however, the group is threatened by overpopulation, non-subjective morality clearly ordains that one abstain from procreation, despite the personal satisfaction inherent in it.

Contraception and sterilization are therefore *moral, neutral or immoral, solely according to the circumstances.*

In order to insure his own survival, man, who is increasingly characterized by his consciousness and his culture, and less and less by his animal nature and biology, must round out procreation with the transmission of his cultural heritage. Otherwise there would in fact be no reproduction of human beings but only of higher mammals. Thus, *a surplus of procreation which may be harmful to the proper transmission of the cultural heritage is immoral.* The maintenance or increase in the number of human beings is justified only if they can be increasingly humanized. It is perforce immoral to increase their number if the result of that increase is to dehumanize them. A group the progress of which toward humanization would be endangered by growth, like a family in which biological, economic or cultural deficiencies might lead to the birth of individuals unfit to receive the transmission of the heritage, should therefore abstain from procreation.

Although the life of a newly conceived child is still only potentially human, the respect owed to that life ordains that its conception should be avoided, rather than that it should be eliminated by an interruption of pregnancy. Like contraception, the interruption of pregnancy may be *moral, neutral or immoral, solely according to the circumstances.* But to justify the elimination of an already conceived life requires more exceptional circumstances than to merely prevent it through contraception.

*   *
*

7. AGGRESSION

From the standpoint of nonsubjective morality, voluntary homicide obviously constitutes the gravest of crimes. It attacks all values. It is an assault on conscious life and on freedom, and violates both the obligation to the species and the social obligation.

In a given number of cases, involuntary manslaughter may also constitute a very grave infraction of morality. If it results from carelessness, for example, for everyone should always take care not to endanger the lives of others, even inadvertently. The driver whose negligence causes an accident is guilty. Likewise, the safety officer whose lack of precaution causes a work injury. It goes without saying that the fault lies with the person who is really responsible and not with his legal representative. Moral responsibility is individual and may not be subrogated.

The deterrence of voluntary or involuntary murderers must therefore be a part of each person's ongoing efforts so as to effectively protect conscious life.

Thus, nonsubjective morality leads to the reevaluation of self- defense and aid to a person in danger, making them into duties. Whoever witnesses an act of aggression against others, or suffers it himself (assault, kidnapping, rape, the taking of hostages, blackmail, destruction or theft of property, etc.) has the duty to try to stop it.

In modern societies, the state undertakes the protection of its citizens, but when circumstances prevent proper recourse to these services, the duty of protection falls upon the witnesses, who by virtue of their presence, are invested with the duties of the community which they represent. Failure to intervene in order to provide assistance to a person in danger is perforce a grave fault, and any violence which must be employed in order to deter the aggressor has nothing immoral about it. Of course, the action of defense must be aimed so as not to exceed the necessary limits of deterrence, but if it became necessary to eliminate the aggressor, the action would not imply a fault, since it would merely arise from the accomplishment of a duty.

In many cases, complicity in a violent act is as grave as the act itself. It is not the satisfaction gained through the aggression that constitutes the fault, but the perpetration of an action against the victim and the assault on conscious life, freedom and the obligations to the species and to society.

From the perspective of nonsubjective morality, the primary goal of punishment is therefore to protect each person from unjust aggression. Punishments must be weighed according to the circumstances, in order to be actually *deterrent*, in the first place, and only secondarily *punitive*. It is from the standpoint of effectively protecting each person that the various goals of punishment must be realistically combined:

1. *personal deterrence*
Its goal is to prevent recidivism on the part of the offender. Therefore, the punishment must vary according to the individual. Whereas life imprisonment for the dangerous recidivist must be truly lifelong, a person who is mentally unbalanced must be helped toward a cure as rapidly as possible.

But the goal of the punishment is to protect both the present and the future. The *sterilization* of recognizably dangerous individuals may therefore be necessary as a matter of morality, if it can effectively protect the group against the proliferation of possible genetic defects.

2. *collective deterrence*
Its goal is to discourage imitators, "correcting others by the one who is captured," as Montaigne wrote. Thus the punishment may be harsher or more lenient depending on whether the group shows a higher or lower rate of criminality, so that it remains an effective deterrent. It is therefore appropriate to widely publicize the severity of individual punishments so that they serve as an example and contribute to collective deterrence.

3. *punishment*
It alone can be "rated" to some extent, without regard to individual situations. Thus some societies, in certain circumstances, may very well eliminate any punitive aspects from their system of correction, provided that their methods of deterrence are actually effective.

*　　*
*

In order to deter a living, conscious being, the punishment must perforce affect both the physical and the mental. It is necessary, therefore, to work on the instincts in order to create the reflex of fear of new punishment, and at the same time, on the conscience, to instill remorse and greater reflection in the future.

To be felt on the level of instinct, the punishment must be applied rapidly. It is doomed to failure if it is not experienced in close association with the criminal act.

For the same reasons, morality dictates that it must be harsh

53

and capable of evoking an unpleasant physical memory. A short but harsh penalty is better than a long but less painful one. It goes without saying, that a repeat offense must bring with it, increasingly dissuasive penalties, since it is proof of the ineffectiveness of the original correction.

Life imprisonment and in some cases, *sterilization* thus appear most likely to protect the group at the level of *individual* deterrence. It is therefore necessary to think of the death penalty not as one of the methods of individual deterrence or as a means of punishment, but as one of the penalties possible in groups in which it is likely to produce a more effective *collective* deterrence than all other penalties.

Within this limit, the death penalty is not immoral. To the contrary, *in groups in which it is likely to better protect the life of each person, its rejection must be characterized as immoral. For obedience to the nonsubjective ethic makes it an absolute duty to protect each person's life, and to deter unjust aggression, above any other consideration.*

SECTION II. HAVING AND BEING

I. ACTION

In order to be characterized as human, an act must originate in the will. For this reason, it always falls within the province of morality. Categorically different from automatism and reflexes, it is the affirmation of a goal, the accomplishment — complete or partial — of a plan.

In human action, it is the psychic universe which dominates. The mind and conscience rely on knowledge of the situation and on an estimation of the direct and indirect, short and long-term results, in order to voluntarily decide.

Thus the human act is the result of a conscious, voluntary and free decision. It characterizes the conscious being. For this reason, the *unmeditated act* constitutes a rejection of human characteristics and a submission to determinism. *The human act must be meditated, otherwise it is immoral.*

Human action involves the entire person. His knowledge, inclinations, temperament, feelings and aspirations are reflected in the totality of his behavior. Any particular act takes on a global dimension from the fact that, when joined to all of the individual's other single acts, it helps to construct a unified personal way of acting. Any judgment that can be made of a man is never other than a judgment of his acts.

The human act requires that reason base its argument on concept, judgment and conclusion:
1. *concept* — the formation of general ideas, which depends essentially on the individual ability to engage in abstract thinking;
2. *judgment* — clear knowledge of a given state of affairs, which depends on the ability to reject common assumptions when they no longer appear to fit the situation;
3. *conclusion* — which depends on the ability to draw a consequence in a logical and orderly fashion.

The capacity for action differs, therefore, according to each person's talents. The ability to grasp the concept, make a judgment and draw a conclusion — whether or not it is directly inscribed in the genetic heritage — depends also on the transmission of culture and on individual development. It can therefore be trained, cultivated and improved.

By inculcating the duty to repay original debts, nonsubjective morality *establishes the duty to act productively.* By establishing the duty to act productively it also establishes the obligation to develop one's knowledge, judgment and will. In this way, it leads each person to establish his own personality. It leads to *being*, by freeing oneself from the alienation of ignorance and submission to determinism.

To be, therefore, is to establish in oneself the specific traits of the conscious being through the use of freedom, in order to overcome ignorance and that which is predetermined, and to contribute to humanization through meditated action.

Thus, from the perspective of the nonsubjective ethic, there is no point in counterposing being and having. *Being* is the primary end, and *having* is merely one of the means to it.

To know, judge and conclude in order to act with the aim of participating in humanization constitute, therefore, the rule of individual self-improvement and the means of establishing one's own personality.

*   *
*

Inasmuch as the ancient Greeks declared that virtue constituted the value of being, and the Romans considered it as the authentic mark of a human being, the virtues arising from nonsubjective morality fit the ancient definitions perfectly. They likewise fit those of the Old and New Testaments, with the single exception that the virtues arising from nonsubjective morality are in no way motivated by the notion of reward or punishment outside the human experience. The gratification which results from obedience to the nonsubjective ethic is limited to the conviction of having taken part in humanization. This conviction is sufficient for some; each person may, of course, add to it the hope of supernatural rewards which are necessary for others.

*   *
*

2. PERSONALITY

Personality is not the person. It is the person with his individual conscience, capable of running his life and choosing his acts. It is the person who has gained awareness of his individuality relative to other values and other personalities.

By obligating each person to establish his own personality through action, nonsubjective morality leads to the uninterrupted acquisition of knowledge, to the permanent molding of character and will, and to constant practice in general ideas, abstract thinking and reasoning, so that each act may be submitted to judgments independent of feelings, fashions and opinions.

It is through his style and character that each individual asserts his personality. It is by making original judgments that he creates his own style and makes his mark; it is through meditated action that he acquires consistency, rigor, indeed, moral grandeur — and establishes his character.

Individual development and self-improvement — and aiding the development and self-improvement of others — are, therefore, essential duties from the standpoint of nonsubjective morality. They include the duty to learn in order to know, to experiment in order to be certain, to act in order to establish oneself — as well as the duty to develop one's gifts and abilities and to reduce one's inadequacies.

* *
*

3. SELF-IMPROVEMENT

According to the nonsubjective ethic, individual self-improvement must not be divorced from its goal, which is to lead to action. The acquisition of knowledge and practice in thinking must be a part of it, and practice in action, an even greater part.

In this type of asceticism — in the Greek sense of the term: exercise, training — the abilities of analysis and synthesis,

57

discrimination, good sense and will are more important than knowledge itself. Its goal is to establish "do what you must" rather than "do what you wish."

Nonsubjective morality thus leads to a demanding asceticism. It requires real training in self-improvement with the aim of leading to effective action:
— through exercising the will, independent of whim;
— through training in general ideas, reflection and reasoning together with conclusions and references to reality;
— through character formation;
— through observation of experiences and analysis of their results;
— through experimentation, risk-taking and action, and also, of course
— through acquisition of knowledge.

The biological heritage, which is expressed through instincts and natural inclinations, is more or less opposed to the demands of asceticism and self-improvement. *Morality leads to marshaling the will and determination to take and persevere in this path of daily self-improvement.* Despite the sacrifices required, it is only through this discipline and asceticism that the human being can be governed by will and guided on the path he has chosen, despite the objections of instinct.

*　　*
*

4. EDUCATION

Natural processes randomly distribute the strong and the weak, the gifted and the incompetent in the realm of conscious as well as nonconscious life. Life is subject to the rule of inequality in nature, and these inequalities are considerably intensified within the human species, where the psychic inequalities of consciousness are added to the physical inequalities of life. The nonsubjective ethic leads to the reduction of injustices through obedience to the principle of equity. Nevertheless, the complexity of genetic laws, which make each person an absolutely unique being, different from any other, forbids any attempt at egalitarian leveling.

To the natural inequalities on the physical and psychic levels, man further adds the inequalities of culture, the rich transmission of which depends mainly on the family, the environment and the society. These inequalities result in the fact that more children of teachers than of workers are admitted to universities, and that, in some cases, whole populations are plunged in illiteracy, while others enjoy rich cultural opportunities.

Despite the fact that observation of modern societies reveals a constant reduction of inequalities in the transmission of culture, the result will probably always be marked by unevenness. Innate differences will always make it easier for some than for others to assimilate the richness of the cultural legacy, and total homogenization of the familial or social environment is inconceivable in a human race in which each individual is unique and each personality is based on difference.

Therefore, to enable each individual to repay his original debts in accordance with his abilities, education must be *differentiated* according to categories of aptitude, so that each person receives the training which can best enable him to fulfill his moral contract. *The dispensing of undifferentiated education is immoral in itself,* for it disregards and sacrifices the real potential of each individual to the illusory goal of an unattainable leveling.

Everyone understands that it would be immoral to provide the same education to the totally as to the partially disabled. But it is less accepted that to the great mass of people culture should be dispensed without excessive competition and without protraction to the point of unnecessarily delaying entry into the work force, while other members of the same population should receive an education based on surpassing oneself and on personal effort by way of *competition* and *selection*.

Any unified system which does not allow each person to give to the fullest is immoral. Any attempt at equalization from above, i.e., generalized elitism, which may discourage a majority of the population not made for competition, should be rejected. In like fashion, any attempt at equalization from below, and all undifferentiated "mass education," should be rejected; neither can serve anyone.

While it is self-evident that in a society possessing few educational resources, it would be contrary to solidarity — hence to the social obligation and to equity — not to first provide a basic level to everyone, it is self-evident that in societies which possess sufficient resources, *it would be immoral not to differentiate methods of education in order to enable each person to give to the best of his abilities.*

*   *
*

5. ACTIVITY

Nonsubjective morality obviously leads each person to choose the occupation in which he has the greatest chances of being effective in his role as participant in humanization. Thus it is immoral to allow chance to decide the choice of a profession or a social role.

Depending on the group, the period and the circumstances, it is more moral to choose certain occupations than others: those which can best meet the group's needs from the standpoint of its improvement.

It would not be in accordance with the principles of the non-subjective ethic to allow only a few the opportunity of usefully contributing to humanization. This process must be the work of an ever growing number, ideally, of all. Thus, the establishment of conditions which can permit the proper choice of an occupation and individual directions and redirections is a matter that pertains to morality.

The simple ancestral action of food-gathering and the sophisticated complexity of automated production are both aimed at the same goals: insuring the survival of the species and participating in its improvement.

In going from food-gathering to stone-carving, man abruptly made his great transformation. Breaking out of the closed circle of mere biological capacities for the first time, he established culture, his true domain. Having insured survival through the transmission of inborn characteristics, which are passed on almost *unchanged* from one generation to the next, he began the process of survival capped off by the transmission of *acquired knowledge*, which is *improved* with each succeeding generation.

A decisive, but fragile victory over determinism — for it meant going from the solid realm of biological inheritance to the uncertainty of cultural transmission. An unprecedented revolution — for, strictly speaking, it created man. Probably a unique revolution — for in going, later, from the broken shard to the wheel and then to the laser, man made only changes of degree within a single system.

By enabling him to tame his environment rather than submit to it, man's activity enabled him to gradually escape the laws of evolution which are governed by environmental constraints. The necessities of adaptation no longer compelled him to transform himself, but only to change his activity. This activity then provided him with two huge advantages: biological nonspecialization — which enables him, for example, to fly without wings through use of the airplane, and to keep warm without fur through the use of clothing — and access to nondetermined pathways. By thus giving him the ability to choose rather than submit, man's activity enabled him to aspire to freedom.

Humanity, then, consists solely of the result of its activity, and morality obviously demands that human activities be directed toward the satisfaction of the true needs of humanization. If we take the case of persistent food shortages, it is obviously appropriate to quit the office for the fields. But the complexity of modern systems of exchange no longer offers such clear-cut situations, and the interdependence of activities hardly permits such simple choices.

Nevertheless, in a general way nonsubjective morality induces man to subordinate purely personal satisfactions and to place a priority on those activities which are most necessary to the evolution of his group. All or part of his activity becomes a service, and one of the essential ways to repay his debt.

In a normal situation, there should be no hierarchy between the various functions which are useful to the group; but if exceptional circumstances arise, a hierarchy is naturally established between those functions which are most useful and those which are less so.

Thus vocations must be weighed. There is no point in choosing an activity for which one has no inclination, but on the other hand, there is no point in striving to make each of one's actions coincide with morality if one's life work — hence, the majority of one's actions — takes a direction which is counter to it.

*   *
*

Absent strong justification, *it is immoral to be a burden to others.* The obligations of the moral contract compel each person to *produce* enough to satisfy his own needs and more.

If circumstances lead to a nonproductive life, it is always possible to compensate for the uselessness of one's main activity by contributing to the collective expenses, by paying taxes or by assuming social responsibilities.

In ordinary circumstances, the principles of freedom and equity perforce give women the right to devote themselves either to a profession or entirely to their family and the raising of their children. This is because raising new human beings is obviously envisioned within nonsubjective morality, as one of the most essential tasks, and as one that best meets the criteria of human activity — provided, of course, that it is actually accomplished in such a way as to contribute to humanization.

Improvement of the group obviously rests on each person's improvement in his or her own activities. Thus, it is a duty to learn new skills and to follow the example of leaders in one's field in order to achieve their level of competence.

In the economic sector, therefore, it is a duty to produce more and better, and to produce necessities first and foremost, with the consideration that in societies which have overcome poverty, to simply produce profits of which a part is used to subsidize collective expenses necessary for social progress is a useful contribution. It is necessary to insure efficiency, obey the tax laws, increase production, improve the results, participate in research and firmly shoulder the risks of innovation.

There is nothing more in keeping with the nonsubjective ethic than to establish, create, develop, invent, improve and succeed in order to contribute more.

6. PROFIT

Work is an application of the personality, an exchange of oneself for a result. It is natural, therefore, to freely dispose of the profit resulting from work. To hinder the free disposal of a gain justly acquired through work and merit is an immoral assault on the principle of freedom. *The right to the fruit of labor and of merit is inalienable.*

The formation of profit is the point at which the group's vigilance must be exerted to insure that the accumulation of profit always results from an activity that is morally irreproachable. Thus, property ownership cannot be accused of being theft. To the contrary, it would be a theft to deny property to a person who had justly acquired it.

If vigilance has been exerted over the formation of profits, there is no way in which their accumulation can be challenged. However, the accumulation of goods, even those justly acquired, can lead to situations which are abnormal as a result of exceptional circumstances and which are likely to place the group in jeopardy or to hinder its progress. In that case, the social obligation may place restraints on the principle of freedom. The borrowing or requisitioning of a portion of the goods held by individuals, which have become essential to the survival of all, may then be justified. There have been too many cases in which collectivization was merely theft carried out without discrimination between justly and unjustly acquired property to fail to emphasize that requisition, even if justified by the circumstances, can only be an exceptional response to an equally exceptional situation.

In ordinary circumstances, an attack on justly acquired property violates the principle of equity. By demobilizing the productive forces, it deprives the group of its most effective incentive from the standpoint of its own development and the most fervent adherence to the social obligation.

Thus, the incentive to work, the protection of the right to the fruit of one's labor, creativity and talent, and the effective control over the formation of profits constitute moral imperatives.

Circumstances guide the choice. In a group whose members are highly motivated by the general interest and sufficiently conscious of the obligations of their moral contract to be satisfied with the fulfillment of duty, the rewards conferred on the creators can be small. However, in a group in which the members are not sufficiently motivated by the general interest, it is necessary to establish systems of incentives which are strong enough to encourage individual initiative in order to obtain a better collective result.

*   *
*

The volume of property is not considered legitimate simply because it is below a certain threshold, whereas above that threshold it would cease to be so. The legitimacy of the conditions under which the profits were formed is the sole determinant of the legitimacy of their accumulation, regardless of their volume.

However, the use to which even legitimately acquired property is put is not a neutral matter. The means afforded by the accumulation of property perforce impose new duties on the owners. On the one hand, since they are capable of giving more, it is their duty to contribute more; on the other hand, a morality based on the repayment of original debts cannot be compatible with the waste of resources which could be better utilized for the advance of humanization. Each person may freely use justly acquired property, but morality tends to prefer a use which is more valuable to humanization and to individual development. It is not opposed, however, to the legitimate satisfactions each person derives from his property; such satisfactions are a useful incentive for all.

In the view of the nonsubjective ethic, property should make it possible to further *participate* in individual and collective development and progress.

Thus, as long as property is indeed an extension of the being which created it, it cannot be despised. To the contrary, from this standpoint, to have the resources which can make it possible to be more and to participate further in humanization is a moral duty.

*　　*

*

Since immorality can apply only to the way in which profits are earned or used, the transmission of property obviously obeys the same rules as its use. Obviously, such a transmission should be aimed at a better participation in humanization, and the natural heirs may represent either the best or the worst choice.

The natural heirs have no more rights over the property which they stand to inherit than the succeeding generation has over the generation which preceded it. This unearned gain substantially increases their debt in terms of the moral conflict. Burdened with additional duties, those who are capable of giving back as much as they have received and more are rare indeed.

But since the right to justly accumulated wealth is inalienable, nothing prevents each person from distributing it as he sees fit. If the natural heirs are not the best choice from the standpoint of humanization, other, more suitable persons or groups should naturally take their place. Such a choice, of course, belongs only to the person who is transmitting his own property.

The obligation to contribute to humanization exists, whether at the individual, familial or national level. This obligation, which cannot be met without resources, compels each person to engage in productive activity. *Thus, from the standpoint of nonsubjective morality, to withhold one's efforts from the creation and accumulation of new wealth is immoral.*

*   *

*

7. SOCIAL INEQUALITY

The realm of the living is governed by the inequality of nature. All beings are different. Human beings are no exception to this rule.

Through their activity and self-improvement, they continually individually create new resources which differentiate them still further. Unequal by nature, and, as we will see later, unequal even in terms of many "rights," men are equal only in their duties. The human species, like all others, is thus subject to the law of the *difference* between its members.

The most effective societies, i.e., those which most fully accomplish their role on behalf of all of their members, are those which best take advantage of their differences and best enable them to contribute in an interdependent way to the outcome of the whole. This is not true for societies of insects, which are mired in immobility, and in which each member is completely subjugated, but it is true for all others, particularly those of the higher mammals, which, like the most equitable human societies, organize the advancement of the fittest through the permanent adaptation of their hierarchy. The natural law of the "pecking order" is an equitable law of advancement without favoritism. In animal societies, it plays the same role as the process by which, in human societies, the most gifted tend to rise to the top.

The obligation of solidarity cannot be reconciled with a social organization that does not take into account the law of differences between its members and does not make effective use of them. Resembling in this sense the law of the "pecking order," equity in social organization must lead to respecting the real ability, competence and results of each person's activity.

Unearned wealth and power resulting from birth, seniority or favoritism at the expense of competence, merit and justly acquired wealth are the product of immoral societies. Morality thus leads to recognizing and respecting the true hierarchy — that which arises from equity.

Equity demands that each person be treated according to his merits. It likewise demands that each rung of the hierarchy correspond to new responsibilities. Whoever receives more owes more. *To reward efforts of value to humanization and deter those actions which are harmful to it are duties of non-subjective morality.* In fact, it is a grave injustice, from the standpoint of morality, to treat those who participate in humanization and those who take part in dehumanization as equals. Its hierarchies are founded on this essential distinction.

SECTION III. MAN AND HIS FELLOW MAN

I. HUMAN RELATIONS

Each person's conduct toward others — not the theoretical conduct between an imaginary self and unknown others, but the real conduct of each personality toward other personalities — constitutes the essential province of morality.

Only the daily relations of each person with those around

him can provide a tangible index of his adherence to the non-subjective ethic.

Conscious life being recognized as the highest value of humanity, the relationships between human beings are necessarily governed by the *equality of respect* owed to each person by virtue of the fact that all embody the same supreme value.

Therefore, nonsubjective morality tends to recognize each human being, without regard to personality and particular merits, as having an equal claim to respect, liberty, truth and equity, independent of race, religion, group or sex. In this regard all men are equal and undifferentiated.

From the standpoint of the nonsubjective ethic, as we have seen, human beings are equal in their duties. When the duties are fulfilled, this establishes certain "rights," in which, once again, all are equal. These "rights" are not inherent in the human personage; they result only from the fulfillment of duties.

That is why equality before these "rights" in no way presupposes that all are equal *in* right. Indeed, while recognizing the equality of all before four "rights" — fundamental, to be sure, but indirect — freedom, respect, truth and equity — we can recognize only:
1. human equality in terms of duties,
2. the primacy of these duties over rights, and, when the duties are fulfilled,
3. human equality before the four rights that flow therefrom.

But this in no way establishes an equality *in* right, which assumes an equality before *all* rights. Duty is based on debt, and right is not based on anything. Let there be no more claims of rights, and nothing changes. But let the fulfillment of duties stop and everything ceases, including human existence. Without respect for duties, there would be no "rights" for the human personage, for the simple reason that there would be no humanity.

Equity demands that each person be rendered what he is owed. But once the fulfillment of duties has established for each person the "rights" to respect, freedom, equity and truth — these rights being equally due to all on the basis of the same value being ascribed to each human being — the moral contract required that they be afforded equally to all, together with the "rights" which flow from them — the "right" to life, progress and solidarity, hence the "right" to subsistence, family, education, work and the fruits of labor.

*　　*
*

In addition to the respect owed to each person merely because he embodies human values, there is the *esteem* which is owed to certain individuals because of their personal merits. This individualization of respect as esteem, this recognition of individual value necessarily differs according to the value acquired by each. Clearly, from the standpoint of nonsubjective morality, it is the degree of participation in humanization which is the main unit of measurement of such esteem; no two persons can have an identical "right" to it.

Honor is the product of merited opinion. It is based on the justified esteem for individual value and may also be considered as the *register* of asceticism. It is directly related to the degree of individual achievement. Therefore, the right to honor cannot be the same for everyone. Once rights have been established by duty, morality requires that men be recognized as equals before some among them, and, on the other hand, that they be recognized as unequal before certain others. Esteem and honor, therefore, which arise from personal values, can be lost, in contrast to the respect which is owed to each human being. And because nothing which is immoral can be honorable, the loss of honor is equivalent to moral death. From the standpoint of consciousness, this is the gravest occurrence.

To guard one's honor through self-improvement, and to defend honor that is unjustly attacked — to expose falsehood and slander, for example — are therefore definite moral obligations.

*   *
*

Respect and esteem are demonstrated through social conventions. In this sense, civility, courtesy, politeness, and, most particularly, sincerity, truthfulness, fidelity and tolerance become duties of behavior.

Sincerity — i.e., the search for truth — and *truth* — that is, a close agreement between expression and reality — are inseparable from a respectful framework of relations. To lie is to disrespect others.

Most metamoralities assert that while nothing forces us always to tell the truth, it is never permissible to tell an untruth.

Nonsubjective morality implies truth as the necessary framework of the logic by which the principles of nonsubjective ethics are applied to circumstances. If the circumstances are not accurately known, the logic would have no value. But in answer to the casuists, who ask, for example, "Is it better to die or to allow someone to die rather than lie?", nonsubjective morality replies that the duty of humanization is not based on truth; rather, truth is based on the duty of humanization. The answer, therefore, depends on the circumstances, the better to apply the principles. A lie that would have stopped the advance of the Third Reich would have been moral.

71

Fidelity, i.e., the agreement of will and action with words and sentiments, is the concrete application of truth and sincerity. It fulfills commitments and obligations, duties and promises. The disloyal and fickle do not meet the criteria of nonsubjective morality. *The moral person is one on whose word others can count.*

With regard to oneself, fidelity means the fulfillment of one's commitments. But loyalty and fidelity are not stubbornness; and when circumstances change, it may be wrong to persevere.

Tolerance, i.e., recognition of the other's freedom to express opinions that differ with one's own, must be absolute, otherwise, like freedom, it ceases to exist. But just as freedom can justify all other freedoms except that of destroying freedom, tolerance cannot accept dehumanization, that is, attacks on freedom, the obligations to the species and to society, and on equity and truth.

*   *
*

Respect assumes tolerance, but truth demands that error be fought. This fight must be conducted with respect for those whose opinion is wrong or whose action is contrary to humanization. Thus, hateful struggle, disloyalty and contempt must be rejected, but it would be a disservice to humanization not to try to repel the attacks on it, and above all, not to prevent their recurrence.

To turn the other cheek when the first has been unjustly slapped is incompatible with the duty to contribute to humanization. *All unjust aggressors must be firmly repelled.*

Naturally, *egotism* and *envy* are outside the norms of conduct arising from nonsubjective morality. To think only of oneself or to feel saddened by the happiness of others is inconceivable for one whose goal is to participate in humanization. Indeed, he cannot help but rejoice at others' success, and if, for the sake of argument, the success resulted in injustice, he would try to repair it through the useful method of equity and not through the negativeness of resentment.

The conduct which stems from obedience to the nonsubjective ethic leads also to treating others as one would like to be treated oneself. It leads, in fact, to the practice of a true, concrete love for others, a love neither theoretical, vague nor generalized, but practiced through daily actions, modified according to circumstances, and leading to giving as well as to scolding or punishing.

Total love, total altruism leads to sacrifice. There can be no doubt that the love created by obedience to the nonsubjective ethic can lead to it in the same way as the commandments of the metamoralities. Like them, nonsubjective morality has its "saints". *They are the ones who have done, are doing or will do the most to push humanity considerably further along the road to humanization.*

*   *
*

2. SEXUALITY

A simple mechanism instilled by nature to insure reproduction, human sexuality nonetheless acquires a special moral dimension. It goes far beyond biological mating and involves the entire personality in its most intimate relations with other personalities. Therefore, it is closely dependent on the rules of conduct.

Relegated to secondary importance by most moralities of opinion, the legitimacy of sexuality was too often limited solely to the usefulness of an impulse leading married couples to procreate. In the process, all other sexual activities were usually rejected as immoral.

73

The sexual act, lovingly accomplished with the aim of pro-
creating and raising children obviously constitutes one of the
most remarkable instances of communion between two conscious beings. It involves them in the most intimate of the
highest values inscribed in the human adventure: creating life
and consciousness through love defined as a total attitude
based on *giving* and mutual *acceptance* of the other's value,
i.e., through the most perfect possible recognition of the
other.

But the majority of sexual relations between couples — married or unmarried — result less from the intention to procreate than from each person's hormonal drives, which, as
we know, vary greatly in their demands from one person to
another.

While there is nothing so remarkable as the willingly pro-
creative act of love, nonprocreative sexuality in no way con-
tradicts nonsubjective morality, provided it does not lead to
the refusal to procreate in a situation where the group is
threatened by underpopulation, and on condition that, out
of respect for the other, all force and aggression — such as
the risk of transmitting diseases, for example — is absolutely
excluded.

In the case of free and conscious adults, only a personal ethic
can place other restrictions on sexual activity, which substantially contributes to the stability of most individuals and to
the harmony of most couples. Furthermore, the willingness
to please and satisfy the partner in order to promote stability
and harmony involves the duty of mutual consideration,
which is not a neutral matter from the standpoint of morality.

*　　*

*

The contract which joins spouses in marriage is clear: it

74

demands exclusivity in sexual relations. But nothing prevents couples, married or otherwise, from deciding differently. In the absence of agreements to the contrary, each person is justified in assuming that the couple is subject to fidelity, on the one hand, and to acceptance of sexual activity, on the other hand.

While one can always get out of a situation that no longer suits him, no one can unilaterally repudiate a contract, be it a tacit one, without doing injury to equity. A person who breaks the contract through infidelity or refusal of sexual activity is guilty, and must accept the consequences.

The responsibilities of motherhood and fatherhood are such that one of the most serious attacks on the freedom of another person is to force him to accept a birth that he does not want. Except for the obligation to procreate so that the group or species may survive, *the will of the person who does not wish to procreate takes precedence over the will of one who desires it.*

It goes without saying, as stated earlier, that the risk of transmitting a defect to one's offspring should lead to abstaining from procreation. The same is true if one does not have sufficient means to insure the transmission of the necessary heritage to one's child so that he may usefully contribute to humanization.

*   *
*

In rejecting all sexual acts not aimed at procreation within the framework of marriage, certain metamoralities were forced to condemn as immoral most sexual practices which, from the standpoint of nonsubjective morality, *may be moral, neutral or immoral depending on the circumstances.* For instance: endogamy, polygamy and polyandry.

Endogamy, which refers to sexual relations limited to the same clan, and, frequently, to the same family — hence incestuous — at first usefully contributed to the improvement of most racial groupings when their characteristics were first established. At one time, therefore, such incest was moral rather than immoral. In other periods, on the other hand, the mixture of gene pools resulted in improvement and incestuous relations were condemned.

It goes without saying that in modern societies, the risk of multiplying individual defects takes wide precedence over the risk of dissolving characteristics, and so incest has become immoral.

Except in case of real demographic necessity, it is clear that *polyandry* and *polygamy* contradict morality by impinging on the equality of the sexes, hence on equity. But they are not in contradiction to it if they are freely chosen by conscious adults.

*   *
*

Onanism, which refers to the pursuit of solitary pleasure, or the accomplishment of the act between married persons without the goal of procreation; fornication, which refers to the act between unmarried persons; homosexuality, sodomy and all sexual activities on the part of the free, conscious and consenting adult — hence, excluding any force, scandal or infringement on the health or personality — as long as they do not involve the refusal to procreate in case the group is threatened by underpopulation, do not pertain to nonsubjective morality, but only to a personal ethic.

The same cannot be said for bestiality or masochism — the pursuit of pleasure through the receipt of pain — or sadism, which is pleasure in inflicting pain — if they lead to brutality or tortures.

Nor does it hold true for necrophilia, which constitutes a negation of the respect owed to human nature. Likewise for pederasty, which refers to sexual activity between a man and a young boy, for even without physical compulsion, there is inevitably an intellectual compulsion resulting from the natural domination of an adult personality over one not yet formed. For the same reason, the heterosexual act is also immoral if one of the partners has not attained a mature consciousness.

Finally, within the framework of nonsubjective morality, rape — one of the most odious attacks on freedom — is perforce a crime which cannot be excused by any sexual impulse.

*   *
*

3. THE FAMILY

By law, a couple without children is not a family.

As we have seen, once the fulfillment of duties permits it, equity leads to granting each person the same "right" to start a family. However, in case of overpopulation, the risk of transmitting diseases or defects, and in the absence of the capacity to prepare one's offspring for humanization, this "right" is diminished by the obligation to the species and the social obligation. Thus, artificial insemination — necessarily neutral from the standpoint of nonsubjective morality — is preferable, for example, to the risk of transmitting defects.

Furthermore, the adoption of abandoned children — provided the adoptive parents do a better job of preparing the adoptee to fulfill his moral contract than if he had not been adopted — is obviously a positive contribution to humanization.

In our modern societies, marriage is the basis of the family, but nonsubjective morality does not require it when it does not demonstrate advantages for the progress of humanization. On the other hand, it establishes the same responsibilities and duties for the couple and for each of the partners whether they are married or not.

The family is the smallest, but the most important unit of society, for up to now, it has been the main vehicle of the transmission of culture, in the sense of "human characteristics." While institutions have generally been able to distribute the essentials of *knowledge*, it is the family which, in all eras, has best transmitted those elements which comprise *personality*: good sense, will, judgment, character and compassion, daily observance of the rules of behavior.

The major responsibility involved in starting a family is enabling the children to contribute usefully to humanization. Thus, the parents fully share in the guilt of their offspring when their actions run counter to humanization. Likewise, they deserve to share in their rewards when they make an outstanding contribution.

The goal of family upbringing is essentially to lead the child to autonomy as an adult capable of fulfilling his moral contract. Since it must lead to asceticism and to individual self-improvement, family upbringing is therefore incompatible with permissiveness. The family must be the place where one learns to overcome genuine difficulties, the harshness of the tests being compensated by tenderness and affection, and freedom being granted to the extent that this training for life warrants it. The parents' duty is to *train their children to become capable of exercising their freedom in a valuable way.* The children's duty to obey their parents is therefore valid until they are truly capable of autonomy and therefore worthy of freedom.

While all animal species show a highly developed instinct to protect their offspring, it is not the same with regard to their forebears. To show one's support, respect, esteem and affection to those from whom one has received the most is a thoroughly human attitude. It may be safely assumed that the degree of humanization of any society and any family is measured by the treatment afforded to those who have outlived the age of productive activity.

* *
*

A couple may fail, break up and separate; the moral implications in this case are many. In dealing with the problems of disagreement, morality demands that mutual respect be maintained and that equity be preserved. Furthermore, it demands that changes in their life together be organized in such a way that their duties to the children are carried out. A separation for the sake of personal convenience in no way frees one, obviously, from the obligation to raise the children to the point where they can contribute to humanization.

* *
*

4. THE SOCIAL IMPLICATIONS

Relationships between man and humanity exist on three levels:
1. the level of the *species*, through the ethnic group;
2. the level of the *communities*: family, school, neighborhood, town, business, partnerships, and
3. the level of *society*, through the state and its administrative and geographical subdivisions.

The species and group are not capable, and, in a majority of cases, communities are no longer structured so as to be able to insure fulfillment of obligations. Therefore, even though they are the product of arbitrary divisions, this burden falls

increasingly on societies, which are set up to enable the group
to achieve its goals.

Therefore, the relations between man and his society differ in
nature depending on whether the society appears as:
1. the legitimate representative of the superior rights of the
species and the group; in that case, it can compel the individual to respect his obligations to the species;
2. the representative of each community and each personality comprising it; in that capacity, it may compel the individual to respect his social obligations;
3. the system adopted in order to best achieve the goals of
the collective entity; in that case, it is clear that it can compel
the individual only in the interest of helping the group to advance toward greater humanization.

*Any constraint by society on the individual which is not ab-
solutely justified by the obligations to the species and the
social obligation and by equity and humanization is an immoral assault on the principle of freedom.*

*   *
*

Thus, societies are tools, and their various forms are justified
only to the extent that they really permit further progress
toward humanization. The pursuit of this goal alone can
authorize them to exert a constraint on individuals.

Such constraints, therefore, cannot apply to the freedoms on
which humanization itself depends, such as the spontaneous
freedom of expression or of creative experimentation, for example, which are the two driving forces of evolution.

We now know that evolution results from spontaneity. It was
through innovation that the metazoon developed into the
human. To refuse innovation is to condemn oneself to the
immobility and paralysis of insect societies. Any social struc-

80

ture which does not give special room to spontaneous expression, to experimentation with new ideas and their adoption, stands in the way of evolution.

Thus, human societies which tolerate excessive social control stand in the way of humanization. By limiting individual initiative, they reduce the chances for creation and innovation and point toward immobility.

But it is the responsibility of societies to give a coherent, lasting shape to the chaos of spontaneous initiatives. A society which could be made and unmade at the whim of its members would lose its reason for being.

Thus, the *authority* and *hierarchy* of societies are justified by the essential coordination they provide in leading the whole to goals which the uncoordinated efforts of each could not attain. They must not, therefore, be elevated to ends in themselves, but should be recognized and respected for reasons of effectiveness. While it is appropriate to challenge and replace them if they prove incapable of shouldering their responsibilities, their principle cannot be rejected without at the same time rejecting the principle of evolution, hence of humanization.

*   *
*

It is up to the responsible authorities to prevent unjust assaults and to deter the social classes which try to obtain unwarranted advantages through force at the expense of other classes. Farmers who bar roads to irresponsible travelers, economic agreements which make use of the embargo, or trade unionists who deprive consumers of energy or transportation are *acting immorally, and must be dissuaded by the authority which the social hierarchy has placed above them. By virtue of the principle of equity, each person retains the right to act in defense of his legitimate interests, but this same principle of equity, and the obligation to respect the freedom of each person, absolutely forbids the taking of hostages as a means of action..*

To defend the classes and groups which are the victims of unjust attacks is as imperative a duty as the duty of self-defense and assistance to persons in danger.

*   *

*

Human societies remain the field of expression of opposing interests and conflicts. We now know that these conflicts are not entirely negative, just as we know that no type of society could suppress them. Observation here proves Proudhon right over Marx: "Antinomy cannot be resolved; it is the source of life and progress."

Conflicts are part of the process of evolution. They cannot be totally eliminated from the process of humanization. That is the reason why means must be applied to make sure that they can always be equitably arbitrated by the representatives of legitimate authority.

*   *

*

5. THE CIVIC IMPLICATIONS

In the framework of nonsubjective morality, a civic spirit is respect for the legitimate obligations expressed at various levels of society. There are municipal civic obligations as well as planetary, regional or national ones.

At each level, by virtue of the moral contract, each person must contribute more than he receives. And at each level to which he contributes, it is his duty to make sure that society fulfills its mission of humanization.

82

A civic spirit, therefore, means both contributing and demanding:

The duty to *contribute* includes the duty of self-improvement and the duty to succeed enough to be able to give more. It leads, for example, to refusing aid except for what is absolutely necessary; to rejecting and fighting interest groups whose sole purpose is to make demands; to refusing excessive guarantees which lead to a distaste for risk and the rejection of innovation and spontaneity.

The duty to *demand* leads to the establishment of an organization, an authority and a hierarchy capable of respecting and compelling respect for the principles of the ethic and the needs of humanization at each level of social integration. It leads, therefore, to making sure that, at each one of these levels, the defense of illegitimate interests is not confused with the defense of the needs of humanization.

A civic spirit further includes *obeying* and *resisting*. While it is necessary to obey legitimate obligations and rules that can insure the process of humanization, it is necessary to oppose those that are contrary to it. It is up to each person to observe the results and criticize them from the perspective of the real short-term, long-term and secondary consequences. To oppose the encroachment of the social on the personal domain; make sure that responsibilities are entrusted to the most competent; reject those who arrogate power and authority without real competence and capacity; put pressure on the authorities to effectively carry out actions which promote humanization — protection of life, security, deterrence of aggression, safeguarding of natural resources, public health, research to improve the health of individuals and the characteristics of the species, improvement of education and training, incentive to individual self-improvement, etc. — these are civic duties which are just as imperative as those resulting from the duty to contribute.

Environmental conditioning weighs strongly on behavior. Thus, a civic spirit should lead to action whenever the environment proves unfavorable to the process of humanization, in order to replace it with a more favorable environment.

*   *
*

But the civic duty is a duty to *participate*. It is not limited to criticism or approval. It is necessarily active, and leads on all occasions not only to approving or disapproving, but also to acting.

The first civic duty consists of really becoming a part of one's genuine communities and societies, to contributing and taking part in them so that they do not deviate from their mission. The duty, therefore, is to participate, but only where one belongs and where one really contributes.

Thus, civic virtues combined with nonsubjective morality lead a person:

1. as a *voter*, to choose officials at each level on the basis of their abilities and their capacity to respect the ethic and to promote humanization;

2. as an *administree*:
a. to denounce infringements of morality arising from regulations and their implementation; to alert the authorities, and, if unsuccessful, to organize opposition;
b. to work to have each official judged on the basis of his results. This holds for elected officials, if each of the voters is vigilant. It also holds for the craftsman, the artist, the inventor, the farmer, the merchant, the businessman, and the producer, as long as each of the consumers is vigilant. But it does not hold, for example, for the civil servant, the journalist, the teacher, the trade unionist or the judge, and it is

necessary to remedy this, just as it is necessary to limit the
areas of intervention of commissions which lead to the dilu-
tion of responsibilities;
c. to accept mobility, when social progress is dependent
upon the transfer of occupations and saturated regions to
new occupations and sparsely populated areas;
d. to act individually by going from the giganticness of the
big cities to the small and medium-sized cities which have
more respect for the individual and his spontaneity; from the
gigantic companies to the smaller ones, from public service
and socializing functions to functions that favor personal initiative;
e. to be successful enough to contribute more, but also to
control the use of tax money, for while taxpayer fraud is immoral and reparation must be made, to allow tax money to
be used for immoral purposes is equally so.

*   *
*

From the standpoint of nonsubjective morality, a civic spirit
leads, therefore, to the continual adaptation of one's own action. One does not act and fight in the same way in the year
2000 as in 1900, whether in the Sahara or in Sweden. When
the majority of the population has only 800 calories a day per
person, nonsubjective morality demands that one act to improve living standards and technical progress; at 2,700
calories, however, it demands more action to improve the
quality of life and social and cultural progress.

*   *
*

6. THE ECONOMIC IMPLICATIONS

Each person's subsistence, and the survival of the group,
depends on economic activity: not only that of the producers,
but in most modern societies, that of the unfit and the inac-

85

tive as well. Well beyond mere subsistence, it insures the means of civilization itself. The support of art and research, as well as social or medical facilities, depends in the final analysis on the results of economic activity. It is, to be precise, the lifeline of social progress, hence of humanization.

The positivist and Mammonite positions, which state that there can be no moral obligations in economics, are, of course, incompatible with a nonsubjective ethic, the obligations of which apply in all circumstances as soon as another person is involved.

Morality leads to seeking the most effective type of economic organization, while retaining respect for the principles of the nonsubjective ethic. Thus, it rejects *pure liberalism*, not because it has had a chance to prove its immorality, but because observation proves that it never exists except in theory. All liberalism always culminates, to one degree or another, in interventionism. It is inherent to liberalism, otherwise it would go towards anarchism. Stemming from utopianism, pure liberalism can be of no use in the search for the most effective type of organization. Furthermore, it is likely that an unrestrained liberalism would led to a return to the laws of primitive animalism, with the strong imposing their will, without limits, on the weak.

Likewise, morality leads to rejecting *economic socialism*, the applications of which have all obviously shown that they led to the repression of freedoms.

Thus the only forms which appear likely to be neutral from the standpoint of morality are those which are most authentically liberal and equitable, those in which the indispensable and inevitable controlling authorities do not obey special interest groups (capitalist cartels and monopolies, single parties or political trade unionism, etc.), but the decisions of an arbiter really situated above them, whose commands are limited to compensating the inadequacies of spontaneity and representing the legitimate interests of the species, the group, communities and persons.

Humanization being tied to social progress, and it in turn being tied to economic effectiveness, the system is necessarily immoral if it leads to rationing, shortages and impoverishment.

More moral, therefore, is the economic system which:
1. makes it possible to produce in less time, with less trouble, more products more in keeping with real demand, thus eliminating waste, unproductiveness and deficits;
2. makes it possible to provide the greatest diversity of products in order to offer a really free choice to everyone. It therefore encourages the taking of risks necessary for innovation;
3. refuses, except in case of otherwise insurmountable shortages, to decide in an authoritarian way what everyone should consume;
4. eliminates the privileges and control of special interest groups, and state monopolies, which are not subject to arbitration and keep the consumer dependent on them; thus, it places competition in the framework of an absolute equality of chances, in order to respect equity, but also to respect real freedom of choice and eliminate scarcity;
5. penalizes unproductive property and rewards productive property;
6. encourages the most effective and useful work by varying remuneration according to results, measured in terms of service actually provided.

*   *
*

The submission of the dominated to the dominant is a law of nature. Man, who is eager for freedom and equity, tries to escape this natural law and thus to oppose man's exploitation of man.

In the distant past, natural submission may not have been immoral. To a certain degree, it contributed to the survival of primitive groups. But in our societies, the domination of the master over the slave, servitude or the exploitation that occurs in factories no longer stem from any kind of necessity. They have gradually become wholly immoral.

However, the compulsions stemming from the need for economic efficiency can never be totally eliminated. Humanization results from collective effort. It has a cost; this cost can only be paid by the organization of everyone's efforts. Although the results should be useful to all, the fact that there is no result without a prior effort means that it is fallacious to claim that the economy should be placed at the service of man, without first establishing *everyone's duty to place himself at the service of the economy.*

Equity, therefore, leads to rejecting economic organizations patterned after nature and based on relations of individual or collective domination; instead, organizations of the contractual type should be chosen. In such organizations, everyone can freely enter into a contract for labor, services, supplies, or to make capital or assets available in order to contribute to the economic effort, without his freedom being restricted beyond what is inevitably necessary.

The basic unit of the economy is the business. From the preceding discussion, it follows that the justification of a business rests both on the production of goods actually in demand and on the creation of profits to be shared with the collective entity in order to contribute to the progress of the whole. While a business must try to insure the comfort, security and satisfaction of its members, it must nevertheless refuse to allow them to consume, whether in payment or in services, all of the profits that it creates. If not, it becomes

immoral by refusing to be placed at the service of everyone
in order to place itself solely at the service of those comprising it.

*   *
*

7. THE POLITICAL IMPLICATIONS

Politics — the art and science of the common good, ad-
ministration of public affairs, and government of the state —
is, from the standpoint of nonsubjective morality, responsible for organizing the functioning of society to help it advance toward humanization.

A nonsubjective ethic necessarily leads to rejecting political
systems which do not respect, or do not command respect for
their own principles, and do not contribute, or lead to effective contribution to the process of humanization.

*Thus, human societies which try to set themselves up as ends
rather than as the means to humanization through the support and coordination of individual freedoms, are immoral
— i.e., those which:*

1. adopt a rigid, a priori description of their form and compel everyone to adapt to it;
2. organize or maintain their members in categories, castes
or classes and tolerate or institute the domination of one over
the others;
3. institute organizational, hierarchical, authoritarian and
centralist constraints above and beyond what is absolutely
necessary for respect of the ethic and of humanization;
4. tolerate giganticness, anonymity, centralization and
bureaucratization which are not absolutely essential;
5. do not insure the separation of powers in order to protect
everyone from their own power.

Likewise, those societies are immoral which do not guarantee:

Respect for freedom, i.e.,

1. complete freedom of opinion;
2. discouragement of attempts to force the adoption of a particular idea at the expense of a diversity of ideas;
3. strict neutrality philosophical and religious;
4. freedom for men, goods, ideas and information to enter, leave and freely circulate;
5. real freedom to create, innovate, produce, undertake, contract, sell, buy, incorporate, hire, choose one's occupation and place of residence;
6. freedom of individual initiative and spontaneous expression, particularly when the society tries to replace this with collective control over management, production and distribution;
7. genuine freedom of choice in all fields — political (votes on the basis of a real choice of candidates), economic, social, cultural, educational, medical, etc.;
8. the establishment of systems which can permit contractual organizations and reject exploitation, servitude and other forms of domination;
9. the institution of genuine competition.

Respect for the obligation to the species, i.e.,

1. providing means which will enable each individual to choose freely to improve his or her health and to limit hereditary defects;
2. maintaining population growth within the real limits of the ability to provide subsistence;
3. peace with the outside world and harmony within;
4. true independence, not only militarily but also of essential goods — for example, grains today for the Soviet Union and energy for France;

5. deterrence of aggression, real protection of life and property;
6. flexibility of structures to permit them to evolve;
7. education differentiated according to aptitude, in order to allow everyone to better contribute to humanization.

Respect for the social obligation, i.e.,

1. real representation of different communities and schools of thought;
2. consideration of different opinions;
3. plurality of choices in order to prevent the imposition of constraints by a single party, trade union, candidacy, art, school or hospital;
4. short and long-term protection of natural resources and of the environment.

Respect for equity, i.e.,
1. adoption of methods to compel everyone to respect equity and the obligations to the species and to society;
2. defense of common interests against special interests, and the discouragement of interest groups which act in an egotistical way;
3. redressing of injustices and wrongs;
4. a system of rewards differentiated according to everyone's merits and results, most especially in the areas most likely to contribute to humanization — the economic, social, political and above all moral spheres;
5. a social hierarchy in which authority and responsibilities are entrusted on the basis of real competence, whatever their origins and categories;
6. changing of officials whenever those with greater competence emerge;
7. the use of effective systems of incentives to motivate the most competent;
8. elimination of castes, classes and other closed categories which claim privileges;
9. elimination of unviable initiatives which incur waste;

10. the redistribution of goods produced, equitably and in consideration of needs directly expressed by the recipients themselves rather than by centralized, authoritarian decision.

Respect for truth, by the establishment of systems which can correct errors and lies.

From the standpoint of nonsubjective morality, a society which tolerates, moreover which adopts and popularizes dishonest theories in order to channel its population in the paths it has chosen, without consideration of the danger to the species, is, strictly speaking, criminal. For example, the dishonest theories of positive eugenics promoted by Nazi Germany, and the hereditary theories of Michurin and Lysenko, which were upheld and defended by the USSR against those of Mendel, at the expense of the truth, solely in order to deceive its people into favoring a particular ideology.

*　　*

*

Thus, the morality generated by a nonsubjective ethic must in principle reject two types of systems which in and of themselves bear the stamp of immorality:
1. *anarchy*, which rejects organization and authority, and thus falls back on the natural solution of the domination of the dominant over the dominated and therefore rejects human characteristics in favor of a return to determinism.
2. *despotism*, i.e., any type of compulsion by an individual, a group, a class or a category.

Morality considers as neutral those types of *socialism* and *controlled free enterprise* which do not socialize or control any more than they have to.

It considers as neutral those types of *liberalism* which do not socialize or control beyond what is absolutely necessary.

92

It considers as preferable those types of liberal socialism and social liberalism which socialize and direct least in comparison with those which give the least genuine freedom to personal, spontaneous initiative.

But within these two types of organization which may, at least temporarily, be accepted as neutral, morality must perforce reject on the level of practice, and according to the circumstances, all initiatives not absolutely justified by the real needs of humanization and not in accordance with the five principle-values of the nonsubjective ethic.

III

A COMMON MINIMUM

1. A COMMON MINIMAL IDEAL

By giving individual acts the mission of contributing to humanization, nonsubjective morality enables everyone to contribute to the supreme project of humanity — advancing in the direction of greater humanization. Thus, action may be inspired by an ideal which is capable of mobilizing energies and legitimizing hopes.

But the ideal consisting of participation in humanization — i.e.,
1. contribution to the predominance of consciousness over matter;
2. contribution to the predominance of freedom and meditated choice over determinism, and

3. contribution to the predominance of solidarity, truth and equity over the indifference of nature,
in no way excludes other ideals, as long as they do not lead to conduct incompatible with nonsubjective morality. The ideal that comes with the adoption of nonsubjective morality does not pretend either to exclusivity. It is simply the common minimum which other ideals cannot avoid if they claim to fall within a moral framework.

Unlike the moralities of opinion, nonsubjective morality does not impose its rules of conduct in the name of an ideal. On the other hand, its adoption involves a type of conduct which can be analyzed as participation in an ideal consisting of the goal of humanization. This ideal, therefore, cannot be placed on the same plane as other ideals. It is not of the same nature. Therefore, it is compatible with them whenever the rules of conduct stemming from those ideals are not in conflict with those which stem from the nonsubjective ethic.

In the same way, a common minimal philosophy may be derived as a consequence of adopting nonsubjective morality without that philosophy having any greater claim to exclusivity. It cannot claim to be all of philosophy. It claims only to be the minimum of all philosophy as soon as one adopts a conduct compatible with nonsubjective morality. A minimum from which nothing can be deducted, but to which one can always add, to reach goals that are considered higher. The daily practice of nonsubjective morality is in no way affected by aiming toward one or another ideal, provided the common minimum derived from the nonsubjective ethic is respected.

For example, the daily practice of nonsubjective morality is in no way affected by adherence to a school of thought which professes the existence of a supreme being governing the universe. It is in no way affected by adherence to the principle that above all else, one must give thanks to or adore that supreme being. It is in no way affected by the principle that one of the means of worship is to not eat pork, drink alcohol, or work on Saturday or Sunday. The daily practice of the common moral minimum is in no way affected by the acceptance or rejection of the doctrine of redemption, the resurrection of bodies, paradise or nirvana, reincarnation or transmigration of souls — just as it is in no way affected by adoption of a Platonic view of the world in which the visible is merely the reflection of a higher supernatural reality, or by adoption of a purely materialist outlook. It matters little, in fact, whether the practice of nonsubjective morality stems from a moral contract considered as the direct expression of human existence, or primarily from an obedience to a higher consciousness from which all else flows, for the simple reason that in both circumstances, it is first necessary to at least respect the minimal rules inherent in human existence. *If a higher consciousness had wanted its creatures to be subject to laws of conduct other than those stemming from human existence, it would simply have created them differently.*

In deriving this philosophical minimum solely from the observable realities of conscious life, and in seeking it as the specific law of conscious life — i.e., in keeping it free of any subjective borrowing — nonsubjective morality inevitably emerged as the first chronological manifestation of psychic expression. The other forms of psychic expression, such as ideals and philosophies, can only be inferred from it, which amounts to saying that they could not but appear chronologically in its wake.

This chronology reverses the usual order of inferences. These generally begin with the definition of an ideal, from which a philosophy is derived, the morality of which is only the practical part of the entire speculative discourse. It is probably helpful to emphasize that the common minimal ideal and the minimal philosophy derived from nonsubjective morality, which are only the consequences derived from morality, itself a mere consequence of the phenomenon of conscious life, thus appear in the natural order of their historical emergence. Our remotest ancestors lived a long time before they could formulate even the most modest ideal and the most rudimentary philosophy — but they could never get along without rules of conduct.

Historically, morality necessarily preceded ideals and philosophy. The nonsubjective ethic restores that chronological order, forgotten for twenty-five centuries.

*　*
*

2. A COMMON MINIMAL PHILOSOPHY

The common minimal philosophy, limited only to what can be derived from the adoption of nonsubjective morality, may thus be formulated as follows:
1. We observe on our planet a phenomenon of conscious life peculiar to man, which may or may not proceed from the will of a higher consciousness.
2. Just as we recognize physical laws as the specific laws of matter, and biological laws as the specific laws of non-conscious life, we recognize morality as the specific law of conscious life, hence of man. We recognize the special nature of this law, obedience to which depends on the will of those to whom it applies, in contrast to the physical and biological laws which are automatically obeyed.
3. Whether or not life and consciousness are endowed with a purpose, we recognize that each living-conscious being has the obligation to act in accordance with morality, its specific law. Failure to do so would result in the extinction of humanity and of consciousness.
4. Recognizing that conscious life is characterized by freedom, and that that freedom permits disobedience to the processes which insure its survival, we recognize that living consciousnesses are endowed with the power to destroy life, and in so doing to destroy consciousness and freedom.

5. We also recognize freedom as the first principle of human existence; if, in certain circumstances, individual freedom can permit one to terminate one's own conscious life, this can only be done with respect for freedom, life and consciousness as principles.

6. The obligation to safeguard and respect the principle of freedom establishes an inalienable, immutable and universal ethic, the principles of which lead to the safeguarding and improvement of the species and of humanity, in the framework of truth and equity. We define human morality as the variable application, depending on the circumstances, of these immutable principles, so that they may always be respected despite the diversity of situations.

7. We call such a concrete morality, directly derived from human existence and independent of all subjectivity, *nonsubjective*. We recognize that this nonsubjective morality constitutes only a common minimum, to which anyone may add — but not subtract — according to his own school of thought and personal ethic.

8. We state that obedience to nonsubjective morality leads to the adoption of a common minimal ideal and philosophy which are compatible with any other ideal and philosophy, provided they do not lead to adopting behavior contrary to the nonsubjective morality.

9. Conscious of all we have received, and of all our debts, and recognizing that man is what he is only thanks to the efforts of his predecessors, we state that there is no such thing as a birthright. To the contrary, man, once he is an adult, has only debts to repay, and is therefore bound by duty.

10. We recognize men as fully equal in terms of their duties, and equally bound to participate in humanization through the repayment of their original debt and more. We recognize that fulfillment of these duties leads to production of means which can be distributed, thus establishing certain rights to which all are equally entitled: the right to freedom, respect, equity and truth. These direct rights also involve indirect rights: the right to life, progress, and solidarity, hence the right to subsistence, family, education, labor and its fruits.

Everyone may, however, on his own merits, create further rights which morality regards as unequally distributed.

11. We recognize also that the human phenomenon establishes a common minimal morality of duty, a common minimal philosophy of duty and a common minimal ideal of duty. Not duty for its own sake, or for mere individual satisfaction, but the double duty to *first repay a contracted debt* and then to *contribute to humanization.*

12. We personally engage in action governed by nonsubjective morality, in order to construct in practice a counter-culture of duty and to substitute it for the cultivation of rights, which by creating illusory justifications for illegitimate demands, turns man away from his path and leads him to disappointment.

13. Consequently, we pledge ourselves to respect the moral contract, that is, to give more than we receive, to maintain in the short and long run the positive values of life and consciousness, to transmit enthusiasm for living and the momentum of spiritual progress; in other words, to try to do as much, and if possible, more, with intelligence and consciousness than nature was able to do with determinism and instinct.

14. We recognize that no theory is useful unless it is put in practice, and we value action as the only way to accomplish duty. We recognize that we are compelled to constantly improve ourselves in order to be able to act usefully. We recognize that the discipline which leads to self-improvement may, for some, be the means of reaching paradise or nirvana, but we recognize that for others it may simply be the means of contributing to the progress of humanization. Everyone shares the common obligation to contribute to this great project, which means exchanging their own existence for something greater. This does not prevent some persons from believing that their action is part of a supernatural plan.

15. Recognizing that ideas make history, provided that they actually put men in motion, and also that the idea which does not lead to action is of zero influence on history, we recognize, however, that the environment which is changed

by action produces new ideas, which themselves are influenced both by that action and by the new environment. We also state the interdependence and mutual influence of action and idea. Thus, we refuse to designate this interdependence as materialism — i.e., to consider it exclusive of all idealism — just as we refuse to designate it as idealism — i.e., to consider it exclusive of all materialism — for the simple reason that, if ideas which arise from new material conditions do not once again drive men into motion, history will stop, just as surely as if those new conditions did not produce new ideas.

16. We recognize also that morality is a property of action, but that action stems from an idea. We fully accept responsibility for our behavior. We therefore consider ourselves the children of our own deeds, regardless of the substantial influences of heredity and environment.

17. We claim individual responsibility for our neglect of duty and accept the obligation to make real amends in terms of increasing our overall debt.

18. Recognizing that in order for evil to overcome good, all that is required is for the champions of humanization to cease to act, we reject the nihilist position which bemoans the fact that "the world which exists does not deserve to be, and the world which deserves to be does not exist." We recognize that there will always be evils to be conquered and that it is our personal responsibility to try to remedy them, beginning with those that are within us and around us. We know that man has his limitations, but we know also that he can accomplish great things, for he has demonstrated this.

19. We pledge ourselves to tolerance in all things, except with regard to those who refuse to fulfill their moral contract. We respect their freedom to choose immorality, but we are opposed to their never giving anything if they wish to go on taking.

20. We recognize as legitimate each person's aspiration to happiness. We note that the definition of happiness is variable and depends on individual assessments. We do not consider, therefore, that the accomplishment of duty necessarily leads to happiness, but we note that it is one of

the necessary conditions. Active contribution to humanization is aimed in particular at bringing the world closer to the conditions which can permit everyone to construct his own happiness.

21. We agree, therefore, that our philosophy of duty is somehow a little selfish because it contributes to the building of our individual happiness in two ways:

1. through the individual satisfaction of accomplishing duty,

2. through the knowledge that by acting for the good of everyone, each person in the final analysis is merely acting on his own behalf.

*   *

*

3. A COMMON MINIMAL CONDUCT

The variability of moral solutions according to the situation renders illusory any listing of rules which can govern behavior in all circumstances. However, a given number of similar situations occur to everyone, so that in a general way, the broad outlines of a common attitude, a *common minimal conduct* arising from the nonsubjective ethic, may be spelled out.

Since we are concerned with a minimum, it goes without saying that nothing can be deducted from it, but that each person can always add to it in accordance with his personal ethic.

The common minimal conduct stemming from the systematic combination of the five principle-values of the nonsubjective ethic may be summarized as follows:

1. to participate personally in the *survival* and *improvement* of the human species, its groups and individuals.

2. to participate personally in the *advance of humanization.*

3. to *improve oneself* through discipline, i.e., through exercising one's judgment, volition and knowledge.

102

4. to participate in the establishment of human societies based on *freedom* for everyone with respect for the legitimate freedom of all.
5. to *repay* one's original debt and *contribute* further, by giving more to the species, to humanity and to one's group than one receives.
6. to promote *equity*.
7. to establish *truth* and *rectitude*.

CONCLUSION

Bergson wrote that biological evolution shows two paths of development: that of the arthropods, which led to a blind alley with the hymenoptera; and that of the vertebrates, which led to the open solution of humanity. The first remained in the realm of instinct, in which everything is natural; but the second, by introducing freedom, introduced the *necessity* of a supernatural law.

This rule, however, is nothing but that which permits consciousness and freedom to endure. It is nothing but the expression of the constraints necessary to insure their continuity and that of the species and of society.

* *
*

The entrance to the kingdom is always narrowest for the "richest." Even in animal societies, the dominant protect the weak, and fight enemies on behalf of the group. They too have more "duties." In these societies, as in the primitive societies of our ancestors, the responsibility of the "richest" fell to the strongest. In societies of slavery and servitude, the "rich" person is the one who holds property; in the most truly contractual societies, wealth is in the hands of those who hold knowledge.

But if strength, wealth and knowledge lead to more duties, they are not, in terms of humanization, what is most useful to develop and transmit.

It is *wisdom* that must be developed and transmitted. And it is parents who are primarily responsible for transmitting it.

As Jean Fourastie has shown, our era has broken with the tradition and continuity to which the raising of children belonged for millennia. For the first time in history, young people are no longer brought up in want, in natural difficulties, in "the visceral fear of need," to use Dennis Gabor's expression. And the absence of real life experience is leading them away from wisdom and common sense.

Knowledge is evolving too quickly for parents to be able to usefully contribute to its transmission nowadays. But it falls to them, and almost exclusively to them, to inculcate wisdom, common sense, will, character and reason. While they no longer need to be the most knowledgeable, they must be the wisest, in order to transmit basic virtues to their offspring. This is the price that must be paid by those who have accepted the responsibility to procreate.

*   *

*

It was Epictetus who first wrote: "The teacher is not there to dispense learned commentary, but to train in words and deeds." The goal is to know what has to be done and to *do it*. Otherwise, what is the use of knowledge? Neither doctor nor philosopher, but actor — that is the role of man, behaving morally.

An ideal of duty, a philosophy of duty and a morality of duty cannot be other than an ideal, a philosophy and a morality of action.

106

Emile Lavielle wrote that all great things are the result of small, slow and insignificant actions. Although not "virtuist," we know that it is not habit that makes virtue, but virtue that makes habit. That is why duty justified action, action that leads to concern for others, for him who "no one will aid if I do not," as Max Muller wrote.

*   *

*

Jacques Ruffie perfectly demonstrated that the processes of life and of consciousness are characterized by complexity. Their constant reorganization is due to the flexibility with which they freely adapt. Self-organization, rich in the autonomy of its parts, enables errors to be transformed into innovation. The incidents which would lead a given machine to jam are, to the contrary, taken over by the gropings of spontaneity and transformed into progress. If rigidity is the beginning of the end, freedom is always the start of the beginning, for it alone is the source of evolution and progress.

But freedom is more than a means. In terms of humanization is it both the *end* and the *means*. History may very well have no meaning — if what is meant thereby is that it is pursuing an end of which each event is a part — but the human phenomenon shows a definite meaning: *that of humanization through the progress of freedom with respect for the constraints necessary to safeguard it*. In sum, that of the gradual distancing from primitive animalism.

In this perspective, there is no distinction between the end and the means. There is no longer *an* end, but an infinity of ends linked together, each of which is only the means to that which comes after it. Each one becomes the means to the next, and so on indefinitely, in the direction of humaniza-

107

tion, the purpose of which is to continue further on the road to freedom, without ever being able to fully attain it.

The restraints placed on freedom in the framework of non-subjective morality are only the consequences of human imperfection. We can dream — but only dream — of a humanity freed of its natural burdens and advancing toward a final, ideal, totally peaceful society.

Emmanuel Mounier wrote that perpetual human harmony is only an infantile dream. The city of men where freedom would reign undivided and unrestricted is mere utopianism. And Berdayev showed that all attempts to construct human harmony have failed and are destined always to fail — historic attempts as well as religious and utopian ones. The great design of morality is not to arrive there either; it is simply to advance with less pain, sorrow and disappointment on the road to humanization.

Whether for societies or for individuals, there is no final moral stage which one tries to reach in order to consider that one has finally arrived. Morality is not only *relative*, it is also *evolutive*. Constantly pushed to higher levels as the demands of freedom and humanization increase, if it were to stop it would die as a result of having ceased to follow the evolution of humanity, which, day by day, moves farther from its original animal nature.

Even if, in terms of the ultimate outcome, nothing leads to anything, we are convinced that the predominance of freedom, solidarity, truth and equity over determinism and the indifference of nature is continually reaffirmed as conscious life frees itself from the grip of its natural origins. We are led to construct our own personality through action, by participating, through duty, in this great project of humanization. It is up to us to draw the satisfactions that come with participation in any great project, even if its objective is distant and is constantly being pushed back. "Joy and serenity are independent of the advancement of the plan," A. Gorz correctly wrote.

The mason need not wait until the last brick is laid in order to sing.